Out of the Blue

Out of
The Blue

The true story of two sisters and their
miraculous survival of one of the most
powerful tornadoes in Minnesota history

Scott Thoma

POLARIS PUBLICATIONS
St. Cloud, Minnesota

Cover photo: Eric Lantz

ISBN 978-0-87839-632-0

First Edition: May 15, 2012

Printed in the United States of America

Published by
Polaris Publications
an imprint of
North Star Press of St. Cloud, Inc.
P.O. Box 451
St. Cloud, Minnesota 56302

www.northstarpress.com

Dedication

To my beautiful daughters Hillary and Heather

TABLE OF CONTENTS

"Every trial endured and weathered in the right spirit makes a soul nobler and stronger than it was before."

—James Buckham

Foreword

by
Jerrid Sebesta

I'll never forget it. The date was July 25, 2000. I was living in Montevideo, Minnesota, when I heard about a tornado warning issued for the Granite Falls area. Knowing the storm was moving away from my vicinity at fifty-five-plus miles per hour, I had to go quickly. I hopped in my car and turned onto the Highway 59 overpass. There I saw it, a dark, low-hanging wall cloud trailed by a white funnel. What I was witnessing was the deadly F4 Granite Falls tornado. I arrived in Granite Falls minutes after the twister hit.

As a TV meteorologist, it's easy to get desensitized to severe weather and tornadoes. We cover them every spring and summer, with most of our time staring at a radar screen, not even seeing the sky first hand. Even video and images of tornadoes and the subsequent destruction they cause becomes routine after some time.

But for anyone who's ever lived through a tornado or experienced the devastating aftereffects, it's anything but routine. I can close my eyes and go back to Granite Falls that night. The smell was that of fresh-cut grass after a heavy rain. Homes appeared to be sandblasted by mud and dirt. Cars and trucks were crumpled like pop cans, littered on the street and in lawns. A fire hydrant was bent over at a twenty degree angle. Mattresses were hanging from trees. Irreversible damage done to a neighborhood and one life lost in a matter of minutes.

After many years of studying the atmosphere and covering severe weather, I'm still humbled by the awesomeness of Mother Nature. There's an amount of wonder and beauty combined with sheer terror of the power that tornadoes display that fascinates me to this day.

My memories of the Granite Falls tornado of 2000 are much like the recollections of those who experienced the Tracy tornado of 1968. Many have lost their lives to these ultra-violent windstorms, but there have been a few, like these young sisters from Tracy, who have literally been in the midst of the tornado and survived.

This is their amazing story.

— Jerrid Sebesta, KARE 11 TV meteorologist

Foreword

by
Seth T. Schmidt

The scars of the cataclysm are mostly hidden. Mature maples and lindens grace once-denuded boulevards. Tidy ramblers, trim lawns, and effervescent flower beds blanket a landscape once pulverized with pathos, rubble, and death. Entombed deep beneath the prairie, the yesteryear wreckage of splintered lumber, shattered elms, twisted steel, and crushed bricks has melded into earth.

Yet memories of the Tracy tornado live on. For many, a portal of awful fascination still links them to June 13, 1968.

Two score and four summers after the colossal funnel dropped from the sultry skies over Lake Sarah, the Tracy tornado continues to cast a spell. Tales of flying boxcars and obliterated school walls are difficult to fathom. The loss of nine lives in the tornado's destruction still haunts us.

Scott Thoma has taken a fresh look at Tracy's hour of trial in *Out of the Blue*, by looking at the tornado through the eyes of two sisters trapped in devastation's path. By going beyond mere anecdotes and statistics, Thoma conveys the wrenching pain that countless people endured — and ultimately overcame — in the tornado's aftermath.

A respected reporter and writer for more than thirty years, Thoma uses his keen skills as an interviewer to add riveting new perspectives to the Tracy tornado story. Readers gain new insights into what happened, and why, on that infamous night. The author's meticulous research also clears up a number of discrepancies and inaccuracies in the tornado's written record.

The Tracy tornado was an extraordinarily rare meteorological event — one of only a handful of F5 tornadoes documented in Minnesota over the past 100 years.

Out of the Blue gives this freak show of Mother Nature's power the treatment it deserves.

—Seth T. Schmidt,
Publisher, *Tracy Headlight Herald*

Author's Note

Because I had been a sports reporter and a sports
editor for a mid-sized Minnesota daily newspaper for nearly thirty years, many of my
friends and family members naturally assumed my
first book would have something to do with athletics.

I was fortunate enough to come across countless stories of interest in my line of work by way of
high school, college and professional athletes and
coaches. I covered two Minnesota prep stars who
went on to play in the National Football League, one
who played in the National Basketball Association,
and even one female running standout who competed
in the Olympics. I also was fortunate enough to cover
a Super Bowl, an NCAA Final Four event, and a PGA
and LPGA Tour event. I interviewed legendary fig-
ures such as Lou Holtz, Tom Landry, Bud Grant,
Arnold Palmer, Walter Payton, Jim McMahon, Bo
Jackson, Wayne Gretzky, and Pete Rose. I had even
played cards with former CBS *60 Minutes* icon Andy
Rooney in a media room several hours before Super
Bowl XXVI at the Metrodome in Minneapolis.

Yet no story I ever came across or any event that happened during my life has affected me like the tornado that struck my hometown on June 13, 1968. It happened in the early evening in Tracy, Minnesota, a quiet city nestled in the southwest portion of the state. I was just nine years old when this powerful beast came swaggering into our town and flexed its muscles. Tightly hugging the ground for several miles, the twister left behind a path of death and destruction.

I still recall the moment I emerged from the basement with my parents and sister after the roaring noise quieted. Almost immediately, the sounds of sirens blaring from emergency vehicles could be heard everywhere. Dogs were incessantly barking. And the wailing of men, women, and children as they emerged from their basements to witness the aftermath sent a chill down my spine. It was as if an intruder had entered our city and stripped us of our belongings. The citizens of Tracy felt violated.

We lived less than a block from where defenseless homes were in the direct path of the tornado and were squashed as if a giant were stepping on a bug.

Once outside following the storm's departure, my father held my hand as we meandered through the neighborhood to see if anyone needed assistance of any kind. He then was called upon to help in a search for an elderly man who had been unable to seek safety due to his limited mobility. As I stood on what was left of sidewalk outside the man's demolished home, I watched as my father and others began removing pieces of rubble in hopes they would find the man alive. Suddenly, my father looked down and noticed that he was standing on a tattered drape that had wrapped around the elderly man like a cocoon. Only the man's hand and the top part of his head were visible. The man was pronounced dead at the scene, yet my father never got over the fact that he had "disrespected" his neighbor by standing on his lifeless body.

My best friend at the time lived across the street from me and was one of seven children in his family. Their house was still standing, but damaged beyond repair. As we walked past his home, I could see my friend sitting in stunned silence with his brothers and sisters on the steps leading to his front door. Usually upbeat during any type of downfall, his somber mood that day has never faded from my memory.

My father, noticing that I had absorbed enough information about life and death for a nine-year-old in one day, took my hand once again and walked me home. Our yard was littered two-feet high with bricks, wood, insulation, glass, toys, clothing, furniture, and books. Only a few patches of green grass were visible.

Later that night, I heard my father come home. He refused anything to eat and said he wanted to be alone for a few moments. He then went into his office and shut the door. You could tell he was exhausted both emotionally and physically by the way he presented himself and by the quiet tone of his voice. I was still frightened from the catastrophic events of this day and wanted to be close to my father. I needed to ask him all the questions twirling in my head. Despite my mother insisting that I leave him alone, I sneaked toward his office. Once there, I turned the knob and slowly pushed the door open about an inch, pressing my face against the opening to see what he was doing. He was sitting at his desk with his head hanging down. As I pushed the door open a little more for a better look, my father's head suddenly turned toward the squeaking hinges. I could see tears streaming down his face. His eyes were red. And his face and hands were as dirty as his clothes. I closed the door quickly and went back into the kitchen where my mother and sister were listening to the news about the tornado on the radio. I never said anything to my father or anyone else about what unfolded in his office, but it was the first time I had ever seen him cry. It shook me up for many years.

Because so many years have passed, accounts of the events surrounding the tornado differ dramatically from one person to another. This made getting the facts more difficult and turned the project seemingly into an investigation. As an example, I counted four versions of a story about a train coming into town just ahead of the tornado. The names of those on the train, where they sought shelter and what type of injuries were inflicted upon them varied greatly, depending on the source of the information. So I had to rely on sources associated with the railroad to get the facts. The same held true with other tornado recollections such as events that went on at the hospital, where lifeless bodies were found and so on. So I started from scratch and visited with many of those people still alive that went through the tornado. If I needed information from a certain source that was now deceased, I attempted to contact a relative, friend, neighbor, or co-worker. I looked up records of those who called in to the dispatcher that day, hospital reports, and obituaries.

One inaccurate story that had been written in several accounts of the tornado was that citizens had to dodge live wires felled in the storm. But sources with direct knowledge revealed that the tornado destroyed the transmitter outside of the city limits, knocking out power to all parts of town. Emergency workers then went around town to test the wires to make sure before informing the public it was safe to walk around.

I contacted employees at the National Weather Service and also the State Climatology Office to learn how the tornado developed and what the weather watches and warnings were on that day. Despite not having the technology that today's meteorologists, storm chasers and weather spotters have readily available, the watches and warnings that day were right on target and likely helped to save lives.

This book is to honor those nine citizens of Tracy killed in the tornado. They were all helpless against this powerful storm and will not, and should not, ever be forgotten.

It's also to honor those who volunteered their services to assist those in need.

And I intended for this book to educate any readers that, unfortunately, may one day be in a similar situation. Showing concern for others by reporting a tornado sighting could save hundreds of lives. Making sure to seek safety immediately upon hearing a warning siren or spotting a tornado may save your own life, or that of a loved one.

Of all the Tracy tornado stories I read or heard about through various sources, nothing intrigued me as much as that of two sisters who were blown out of a house and survived. Unfortunately, a two-year-old girl also in the home was not as fortunate. Trying to picture the sisters being thrown around outside like rag dolls while not being struck by the vast number of missile-like objects launched by the tornado's fury was unfathomable to me.

The siblings' story of survival was powerful and compelling to me. I always thought it would make an interesting non-fiction book. Like other books I had attempted to write before and abandoned due to time constraints or boredom, I figured this book would also never come to fruition.

Then came a tap on my shoulder . . .

Out of the Blue

Chapter 1
HOME AGAIN

Summer 2011

IT HAD BEEN OVER FIVE YEARS since my father passed away following a heart attack, and I had only been back to my hometown of Tracy, Minnesota, a few times since then. My mother passed away in 1999, and it was always troubling for me to retrace the steps of my childhood. We were a very close family and by purposely staying away, it was easier for me to remember their lives and not their deaths.

On one potentially stormy day in mid-July, I convinced myself to start facing reality and return home to visit my parents' final resting place, as well as to seek out some of my childhood friends, neighbors, former teachers, and coaches who I hadn't seen in a long time.

I'd lived in Willmar, Minnesota, ever since I graduated from high school and left home in 1977. Willmar is located approximately eighty-five miles northeast of Tracy in the west central part of the state. The two cities were close enough that an occasional ninety-minute drive would keep me connected to the town I grew up in. Yet I kept my distance in recent years as if the cities were on opposite sides of the country.

I took Minnesota State Highway 23 west out of Willmar, traveling through the towns of Priam, Raymond, Clara City, Maynard, Granite Falls, Hanley Falls, and Cottonwood before turning south for nine miles on County Road 9, then east for three miles on Minnesota State Highway 19, before a final fifteen-mile straight stretch south on County Road 11 into Tracy. County Road 11 was always referred to as the "Airport Road" by residents of Tracy. Rarely did they use the actual road number in a conversation. Instead, "He lives about four miles north on the Airport Road" or "Take the Airport Road about nine miles north and then turn right . . ." were typical directional references.

As I was closing in on Tracy, an unwanted sound outside the vehicle began overtaking the radio voice I was listening to. Before I even had a chance to turn the volume control knob down on the radio, the *karumpfff, karumpff, karumpff, karumpff* reverberation and the vehicle's desire to pull toward the passenger's side shoulder of the road made it understandably clear that I had a tire in desperate need of inflation.

Naturally, the rain starting coming down simultaneously with the WCCO radio voice's forecast calling for precipitation in southwestern Minnesota. "No kidding?!?" I said aloud, aiming my sarcasm in the direction of the radio as if the meteorologist would apologize or suddenly make the rain stop long enough for me to change the tire.

The drops weren't coming down hard, nor were they large enough to splash against the windshield once they made contact. But it was enough of a rain that I knew I was about to get wet. Because of lightning consistently streaking across the sky, the radio was filled with static. Still, the meteorologist seemed to be mocking me with his announcement calling for the potential for heavy showers in the area. I knew I had better attempt to give my best impersonation of a pit crew member and get the flat fixed as quickly as possible.

Once I stepped outside the vehicle, a quick inspection revealed that the front passenger tire wasn't completely flat, but was low enough that I didn't want to risk driving the remaining five miles into Tracy to inflate it. Besides, the tire looked like a doughnut with a bite out of it so I figured the rim would chew into the rubber if I drove any further. Not only would I have to purchase a new tire, I'd likely damage the rim, too. It was strange that a flat would occur at this point, eighty miles into the trip. I didn't recall running over any glass or sharp objects. And the tires on my vehicle were less than a month old. It was also strange that I chose to wear tan Dockers and a short-sleeved white shirt on this particular day, both colors that were going to attract dirt like a magnet over a pile of paper clips.

After removing the flaccid tire that spelled out Goodyear in white raised letters from my Chevy Blazer, I replaced it with an antiquated spare that looked like it had been hanging from a rope in an old willow tree for generations. It looked out of place in comparison to the other three tires, but would serve its purpose of getting me into town.

Dirty and damp, I tossed the jack and the deflated tire into the back of my vehicle. Before getting inside the vehicle, I stood on the side of the road while peering across the countryside. In all the years I lived in the area or visited, I never really had stood in the countryside at this location. The first thing I noticed was how flat the land was in all directions. I could see for miles.

After brushing off as much dirt and grime as I could, I grabbed a metal sign post stationed on the shoulder of the road with both hands, partially bending over to allow my lower back muscles to stretch a little. As I let go of the sign to stand back up straight, I immediately recognized the sign. I had passed it hundreds of times en route to Tracy over the years, but never gave it much thought. It was a green mileage sign. The top line read: "TRACY 5" in white letters with an arrow pointing up to indicate the direction of the town was straight ahead. Below that was marked "AMIRET 4" with an arrow pointing to the right, or to the west of the direction I was headed.

"Wasn't this the spot where a Tracy baseball team was riding home in a school bus and witnessed the tornado terrorizing Tracy in 1968?" I asked myself. I had recalled someone mentioning it to me several years ago, but the details were unclear to me now. I attempted to visualize how the bus driver, coach, and players could see the churning from this distance, then realized that with the land so flat in this area something that size would easily be visible.

I have always been fascinated with tornadoes and how that much power can be generated by two fronts with contrasting temperatures meeting. I likened the collision of these fronts to the Civil War when mass units of Blue and Gray soldiers, similar colors of storm clouds, would charge at one another in an open field. When the battle was over, smoke hovering a few inches off the ground was eerily blanketing the death and destruction left behind . . . just as the tornado that charged through Tracy over forty-three years earlier.

The rest of my drive into town was spent thinking back to that June 13 date. My mind conjured up a mental picture of the demolished elementary school I had attended and wondered if anyone ever saved any of the bricks for posterity's sake. I wondered if any of the trees still held tattered pieces of cloth that would wave in a breeze as if the entire town were surrendering. I thought about the nine people killed that night and how frightened they must have been prior to their death. I had lived in Tracy for nine years following the tornado, but gave it little thought after the town was cleaned up. I knew there was a memorial along Highway 14 for those killed in the tornado, but now I wanted to examine it more. Now that I was older, it would likely have more meaning.

And then I thought about the two sisters, Linda and Pam. Linda was twenty years old when the tornado struck. Pam was eight years old and a year behind me in school.

I heard so many variations of the story of their survival over the years that I wondered which one was factual. As I drove a mile south of Tracy to visit my parent's grave site, I passed the area where Linda and Pam were the night the tornado hit. There was no way now to tell a tornado had ever leveled the area. The majority of the homes in this area had been destroyed, and now the site was filled with new homes.

A multitude of questions regarding the sisters began popping into my mind like a bag of microwave popcorn in its latter stages of cooking. What was it like being tossed around like a tumbleweed? What did they see? What did they hear? What did they feel? How far were they blown? Are they now terrified when severe weather approaches?

I just had to find out.

Chapter 2
COMING TOGETHER

June 1966

FATIGUED AND COVERED WITH CHICKEN fat and blood from head to toe after the first day on the job, Linda Haugen wondered if she had made a wise decision by accepting a job at a business with less than comfortable conditions. Co-workers laughed aloud and assured the rookie worker that, as time passed, she would get used to the smell, the cold, and even the greasy parts of a chicken.

When Linda graduated from Tracy High School in 1966, there had been little money available for her to attend college. As the oldest of the six children of Clarence and Betty Haugen, Linda grew up in a modest Minnesota environment and figured the sooner she could make it on her own, the better it would be for everyone. Linda had very little desire to attend college anyway. She had her sights set on saving enough money to buy some type of a vehicle and travel around the country to take in sights she had only dreamed of visiting before.

Just three days after grabbing the tassel on the right side of her mortar board and shifting it to the left after receiving her diploma from Bruce Govig, the school superintendent, Linda told her parents it was time for her to abandon the nest and fly solo. Her plan was to move to Worthington, get a job and then take life one day at a time after that. There was no particular reason why she chose to live in Worthington, then a growing Minnesota community that lay sixty miles south of Tracy and only ten miles north of the Iowa border. Linda had no close relatives in Worthington, nor did she have any friends there who had influenced her decision. This was simply a young woman making a stab-in-the-dark selection.

Linda's parents knew their daughter was ready to be on her own. She was mature for her age, street smart and unafraid of taking chances. Some friends and family members attempted to talk her out of such a spontaneous venture and pleaded with her to stay at least until the end of the summer. Even though it was a quick decision to leave, it wasn't made because she needed to get away from anyone in particular. Nor was it that she detested the town she lived in and couldn't wait to get out of there, ala many post-high school students. Starting life on her own with no plans and little money in an unfamiliar community was more of a challenge to Linda than a gamble. She had to start somewhere and Worthington seemed as good of a place as any.

Linda couldn't wait to make decisions on her own, basking in the enjoyment of the right ones while hoping to learn from the wrong ones. But Linda's parents were both working and unavailable to drive her to Worthington at the drop of a hat. It had been only a week since graduation, yet Linda was ready now. So rather than waiting until they had an opportunity to transport her, the anxiety-stricken teenager placed a call to a taxi company in Worthington to pick her up in Tracy and bring her back to Worthington. The driver's round-trip fee would come to twenty-eight dollars. Even before she had started her independence, Linda was learning how fast money evaporated. The only things Linda took with her in the taxi that day were her clothing, a few personal mementos, and her purse that contained 175 dollars in cash, including sixty-two dollars that she had received in graduation cards.

Linda hadn't bothered to call ahead to reserve a hotel room, nor had she even arranged for a place to stay that night in Worthington, a town with a population of 9,600. She asked the taxi driver to let her off in front of the Worthington Hotel. Linda then reached into her purse, pulled out her money and counted out what she owed. She leaned over the front seat and placed the cash in the driver's hand, thanked him and stepped out of the vehicle.

As soon as her feet were firmly planted on the ground, Linda felt much older than eighteen. She was alone now with no one to guide her. She paused in front of the hotel, staring at the front door. After taking a deep breath and exhaling through her mouth in an attempt to settle her nerves, Linda then walked inside the hotel, headed over to the reservation desk and secured a room for a week. The price for a one-night stay was fifteen dollars, but a booking for a week was seventy dollars. So she loosened her purse strings once more. She had only been in Worthington for five minutes and had already spent over half of all the money she had to her name.

After putting her clothes in the hotel room's three-drawer dresser, Linda walked to a grocery store to purchase a few food items and the current edition of the *Worthington Daily Globe*. On her walk back to the hotel, she perused the classifieds section of the paper for job openings. Once back in her room, she took out a pen and circled any jobs that seemed interesting or manageable. She wasn't going to be particular about the job selections. Any offer would suffice for the time being. Even if she wasn't happy at the place of employment, she would stay until a better offer popped up.

Linda awoke early the next morning, eager to get started in her job search. With her money dwindling quicker than expected, she needed to start replenishing her funds as soon as possible. With the newspaper tucked inside her purse, Linda set out on foot to find the locations of the six businesses in town she had circled. The hotel she was staying at was only three or four blocks from the majority of those businesses. She had no trouble finding each of them and proceeded to enter each building and fill out an application. When the application posed the question as to when the applicant could start work if hired, Linda wrote, "Immediately." A few other businesses she passed not currently advertising for help also piqued her interest. So Linda went inside each of those businesses to inquire about any possible job vacancies.

Three days after she had applied for a job, Linda was offered a position with Campbell's Soup Company in Worthington. She readily accepted and was asked if she could come to the company that day to fill out some employment forms. Linda practically left skid marks on the sidewalk outside the hotel as she hurried off to learn what her duties would be, how much money she would earn and when she could start working for them. The boss informed Linda that she would be paid the Minnesota minimum wage of $4.90 per hour if she wanted a daytime shift or $5.10 if she worked the night shift. which would be from 3:00 p.m. until midnight, Monday through Friday. Linda chose the night shift in order to make as much money as possible and move into an apartment.

At Campbell's, the largest soup maker and marketer in the world, Linda was assigned to the eviscerating department where chicken carcasses were kept once they were defeathered and had their heads and feet removed. The room where she worked with fifteen others was kept at sixty degrees Fahrenheit. Many of the company's line of soup products manufactured at the Worthington plant included chicken — among them was chicken noodle, chicken and rice, chicken vegetable, cream of chicken, chicken gumbo, chicken broth, and chicken dumpling soup. Linda and others in the eviscerating room were required to disembowel the birds. A small slice would be made to open the back end of the chicken and workers would reach a gloved hand into the cavity of the bird as far as they could. They would then curl their fingers downward to grab a handful of viscera and internal organs and carefully pull their hand back out to remove them. Each worker had to be careful so as not to burst the chicken's gall bladder. If the gall bladder was damaged, bile would leak out and contaminate the meat.

Chickens had to be chilled to below forty degrees Fahrenheit within four hours of death. So workers in the eviscerating room had to disembowel the birds quickly and carefully before placing them in buckets of ice water.

Disemboweling a bird was tedious and tiring work with little reward. After all, extracting guts out of a chicken isn't among the most glamorous jobs in the world. Workers would stand next to each other for hours at a time, their hands buried up to their wrists in the rear end of a chicken. The insides of the chickens would then be tossed into huge tubs in various locations on the floor. After working for a short while, the workers' hands would get cold and less nimble, making the job even more difficult. Employees working in the eviscerating room would dress warmly, then wear white full-length plastic aprons over their clothing. They also wore hair nets and rubber gloves. By the end of the day, blood and slimy yellow fat were covering most of their uniform fronts.

When a worker returned home at the end of a shift, a hot shower felt like a reprieve from the governor.

Because of the close proximity to one another in the line, workers quickly became familiar with one another. They would tell each other about the positive things in their life, as well as the negative. They would talk about relationships, medical problems, vices, pet peeves and other personal information. Some were more close-mouthed when it came to personal issues, while others were an open book.

Following one full week of working at Campbell's, Linda had earned enough money to move out of the hotel and put a deposit on a rooming house room only three blocks from her work. The owner of the rooming house was an elderly woman who lived on the main floor. She had no strict rules and charged the tenants seventy-five dollars per month to live there. There were three rooms on the upper floor, each vacated by a young lady. The rooms included a couch, end table, lamp, small refrigerator, hot plate, kitchen table and chairs, bed, and a television. Similar to a dorm, the girls shared a bathroom on the upper floor. Until she got acquainted with some of the townspeople, Linda spent most of the time outside of work in her room reading or watching television.

Linda worked on the eviscerating line for four weeks before she was moved to the deboning line. It was harder work, but she earned ten cents an hour more than she was previously making in the eviscerating department. Deboning a chicken required a steady hand and a sharp knife. In order to prevent workers from accidentally cutting their fingers, Campbell's provided them with mesh steel work gloves. The gloves were flexible, but sturdy enough to stave off razor-sharp knife blades. Crew members would be required to cut away the bones from the meat at a steady pace. Uniforms were the same as those worn on the eviscerating line except for the gloves that looked like those used by a knight about to joust.

Linda soon began building a friendship with Clifford Vaske, who also worked the night shift on the deboning line. Clifford was five months younger than Linda and had just graduated from high school in Adrian, a small town eighteen miles west of Worthington. Clifford commuted to and from work each day from his family's farm fifteen miles away.

The two teenagers started taking breaks and eating lunch together, and it was becoming obvious to others that there was a mutual attraction. After getting over the awkward flirtatious stage in their relationship, Clifford and Linda agreed to spend time together away from work. With neither of them having much money, the first date consisted of watching a movie on the television at Linda's place inside the boarding house.

With fall nearing retirement for 1966, the advent of winter was beginning to force the mercury southward. So Clifford would pick up Linda in his car each afternoon for work and drop her off upon completion of the night shift. Clifford drove a 1960 candy-apple red

Ford Thunderbird that he bought for 800 dollars after graduation. He was proud of the car and took exceptional care of it, washing and waxing it as soon as a speck of dirt dared to settle anywhere on it. Linda thoroughly enjoyed going for rides in the Thunderbird and often noticed envious looks the car would generate from passers-by.

Another worker stationed on the deboning line, Susan Vlahos, had become friends with Linda and Clifford. Susan was a twenty-one-year-old single mother with a six-month-old daughter. She had given birth on January 8 in a home for unwed mother's in Sioux City, Iowa. She named the girl Nancy Ann Vlahos.

When Susan was pregnant, she was living with her parents in her hometown of Hampton, Iowa. But Susan's parents were unable to accept the fact that they had an illegitimate grandchild and told Susan to move out if she chose to keep the child. Susan did not want to give the child up and decided to seek employment and move away. She and a friend saw an ad for job openings at Campbell's Soup Company and each applied. Two weeks later, they were both hired and roomed together in Worthington.

It wasn't long after Nancy was born that Susan came to the realization that motherhood was not her forte. She was unaccustomed to being strapped down. She enjoyed the freedom of going out with her boyfriend, Earl, also Nancy's father, and her other friends. Susan didn't have the money to pay a babysitter and would find herself sitting at home on weekends while her friends were living the carefree lifestyle she had enjoyed before becoming a mother.

Linda, who loved children and was accustomed to caring for them from her days living at home with her siblings, volunteered to watch Nancy one Saturday night. Before the words had a chance to escape Linda's mouth, Susan was excitedly accepting the offer.

Susan was outgoing and friendly. Co-workers got along well with her and enjoyed her offbeat humor. But it was easy for everyone to see that she wasn't ready for motherhood. It's common for a mother to provide a daily analysis of her baby's progress to anyone within earshot. She would detail things such as when the baby rolled over, took a first step or said its first word as if she was impersonating a football play-by-play announcer. And many of those being told the information repetitively would pretend as though they were interested by issuing a polite smile and nod every so often. But Susan rarely spoke about Nancy or any of the activities the two of them did together unless it was to impart information about the financial struggles of being a single parent. Susan talked more openly to co-workers about parties she had attended or silly things she and friends had said and done than she did her own child. And she never spoke to any of them about her baby's father. Not even Linda, who spent a lot of time with Susan and confided in her regarding personal matters, had ever heard Susan mention the baby's father.

There was a valid reason why Susan didn't bring Earl's name up. A few weeks after Nancy was born, Earl was injured working on his car. With the engine running, Earl leaned in too far and the fan clipped him in the face. He was rushed to the Sioux Falls hospital and was in critical condition. On February 16, Susan's twenty-first birthday, Earl passed away from his injuries. She rarely spoke to anyone about the accident after that.

Susan's apartment was within walking distance of the boarding house where Linda rented her room. It was cold outside, accented by a brisk November wind. Linda pulled the collar of her coat up to block some of the breeze blowing against her ears. As she walked, Linda felt excited about having the opportunity to care for a child again. When Linda saw Nancy for the first time, it triggered memories of being back home with her siblings, Kathy, Chuck, Pam, Georgia, and Abbie. Linda had a fondness for children and enjoyed interacting with them. Since leaving home, the opportunity for Linda to be around children had not presented itself.

When Linda met Nancy for the first time, she immediately thought about how exciting it was going to be to have children herself some day. Nancy was an adorable child. She had blonde hair, blue eyes and an engaging personality. She seemed like a happy child, always sporting a wide smile. And she had an enormous amount of energy. As she was nearing her first birthday, Nancy was beginning to take steps on her own. Like most toddlers in the inaugural stages of walking, Nancy wobbled around like a dizzy penguin. After Susan left the house to meet with some friends, Linda got on the floor with Nancy. She rolled a ball to the girl, making her laugh aloud each time it would softly bump into her legs. After playing together for a while, Linda read Nancy a story before tucking her into bed for the night. Looking at the toddler lying in her bed made Linda again turn her thoughts to being a mother. Even though she had spent only a short while with Nancy, Linda felt an unexplainable closeness to her.

Returning to her rooming house later that night, Linda felt a pang of sadness and anticipated the next time she could be with Nancy. When Linda went to bed that night, the image of the little girl would appear every time she closed her eyes. Linda knew Susan was not the motherly type. In fact, Susan herself felt the same way. So Linda toyed with the notion of taking care of the girl more often. Linda had not been offered, nor was she expecting, any pay for her babysitting chores.

At work on Monday, Linda presented Susan with the idea that she would babysit more often. Susan offered no resistance. So Linda began frequenting Susan's house on weekends so often that she was staying overnight on occasions. That also allowed Susan to remove the shackles of motherhood more often and enjoy the lifestyle she had been missing since giving birth.

Because Clifford and Linda were spending so much time together and neither of their pockets were overflowing with money, they felt moving in together was the best option. There were several factors that they based their decision on. Clifford wouldn't have to drive thirty miles round trip each day to Worthington. They could pool their money and enjoy some of the things they could not currently afford. They each would have more room than the place they were living in. And, most important, the could spend even more time together.

The bond they were developing with the little girl was also bringing Linda and Clifford closer together. They were now seeing each other on a regular basis and within a few months of meeting for the first time, had decided to move into an apartment together. With their own place, Linda and Clifford began to bring Nancy over on weekends. The girl was fast becoming an important part of their lives. They loved being around her and couldn't wait until the weekends to spend time with her. But they wanted her to be with them always. Susan knew she wasn't going to be a good mother and that the little girl deserved a better home. Linda would make a much better mother for Nancy, Susan felt.

When the spring of 1967 unfolding, Clifford and Linda mutually agreed to get married. The couple had talked about it often, and they both felt ready to take the plunge. Linda had turned nineteen years old on April 25 and was fully prepared to become a wife and a mother. Linda and Clifford met with Susan and asked if they could adopt Nancy. The mutual understanding was that Clifford and Linda would bring

Nancy into their home as a foster child as soon as possible and then eventually legally adopt her after they were married in August. Susan always wanted Nancy to have good parents and with Earl's death, she felt Linda and Clifford were the obvious choice. She knew they would make wonderful parents, especially after watching how much love they showered Nancy with.

Clifford would not turn nineteen until September 11 so he needed parental consent under Minnesota law to get married. But Clifford's parents, Virgil and Dolores, felt their son was too young to get married and did not grant him permission. Partly out of bitterness toward his parents, Clifford told Linda that he didn't want to wait one more month until he turned nineteen so he checked the state law in Iowa for the legal age required to get married. After all, he figured, the Iowa border was only twelve miles south of Worthington. But he soon discovered that Iowa's age requirement for marriage was the same as Minnesota's. And it was the same in Wisconsin and North and South Dakota—other states surrounding Minnesota. Even Nebraska had a similar law. But Clifford kept trying and found that Michigan only required parental consent if either party was seventeen years of age or younger. The state of Michigan's northwest tip was closest to northern Minnesota with Wisconsin sandwiched between the two states. Clifford checked an atlas and located a small town called Bessemer just a few miles across the Michigan border. He figured the trip from Worthington to Bessemer would takes around eight hours by car.

He also noticed that Bessemer was the county seat in Gogebic County, so Clifford called ahead to arrange for the Justice of the Peace to marry them. Even though Nancy was now spending the majority of her time at the Vaskes' home, she would stay with her mother while Clifford and Linda eloped to Michigan.

With little money and free spirits, the couple planned to make August 15, 1967, their special day. Clifford gassed up the Thunderbird and checked the oil before he and Linda took off down the highway on their 400-mile journey to matrimony.

Once in Bessemer, the couple located the courthouse and within minutes were pronounced husband and wife. Neither of the newlyweds had much money so the trip to Michigan also represented their honeymoon. The couple ate at a local diner in downtown Bessemer, then secured a room for the night in a hotel.

The next morning, Clifford and Linda returned to Minnesota and, a month later when Clifford turned nineteen, renewed their vows in a quiet ceremony in the Catholic Church in Worthington.

Clifford and Linda cared for Nancy every day and filed for adoption with the State of Minnesota.

With the Vietnam War nearing its thirteenth year, Clifford was drafted into the U.S. Army in April 1968. Before being shipped off to Fort Lewis, Washington, for basic training, he and Linda decided to move to Tracy. They drove to Linda's hometown on two separate occasions to look for a place to rent. They eventually found a modest home owned by John Holbrook in Greenwood, a suburban section on the south edge of Tracy, that they could afford and was the perfect size for them. As soon as the first month's rent was paid, Clifford and Linda quit their jobs at Campbell's.

Susan packed all of Nancy's belongings and the Vaskes loaded them in a trailer they had borrowed. There was no lengthy goodbyes between the biological mother and her daughter. Because the girl had already been staying with Clifford and Linda for several months already, it was as if they were already her parents.

The Vaskes' new home sat on the corner of Greenwood Avenue and Adams Street. There was a large weeping willow tree in the front yard, as well as a white picket fence. The one-story house had only five rooms: a living room, kitchen, bathroom, master bedroom, and a small second bedroom. The basement was unfinished, but it included an old-style washing machine with a ringer attachment. There was no garage, but there was a small shed in the backyard. The house was the perfect size for the three occupants. Having a small bedroom next to the master bedroom allowed Nancy to have her own room, yet still be within earshot of Linda.

Living in Tracy now enabled Linda to be near her mother and siblings who lived in the Broadacres section just under one mile east of Greenwood. Her parents had divorced shortly after Linda left home, and Clarence was now living near the business section of Tracy. Although Linda never regretted leaving Tracy, she was happy to be back in her hometown. There was a certain comfort level that she didn't have in Worthington. Now married and having the responsibility of caring for a child, Linda figured that was what had been missing from her life when she was so anxious to leave home in the first place.

With Clifford leaving in May of 1968 to fulfill his military obligations, the Vaskes temporarily put the adoption paperwork for Nancy on hold. The couple had been married only nine months and under Minnesota law at the time, needed to be married for one full calendar year in order to finalize the adoption process. Nancy had already been living with the Vaskes for five months when Clifford left for the service. To the Vaskes, Nancy was their daughter, and it was only a matter of time before it would be made official. Even in a town where it seemed everyone was aware of the latest events, many assumed Nancy was already Linda and Clifford's daughter. If Linda took Nancy along to the grocery store or some other outing, oftentimes an acquaintance would greet them and ask Linda how her daughter was.

Like a proud mother, Linda would politely respond without explaining that Nancy was not yet officially her daughter.

Chapter 3
A RAILROAD TOWN

L IFE IN A SMALL TOWN IS NOTABLY different than the fast-paced lifestyle of a big city. There is far less congestion, easy access to parking during shopping excursions and little, if no, waiting in lines at a bank or post office. But because of limited resources, modest cities also must attempt to manufacture their own means of entertainment. And business owners must enhance sales through means such as friendship, trust, and ingenuity in order to prosper.

Growing up in Tracy was often uneventful and predictable, yet comfortable and uncomplicated. The comfort of the town was one of the reasons why Linda chose to return after her brief stay in Worthington.

The population of Tracy hovered around the 2,500 mark over the first eight decades of the twentieth century. And because few families left or arrived each year, it seemed as though one knew just about everyone else in town and also what each other's business was, whether a person wanted to or not. If someone bought a new car, chances were that, by the end of the day, residents on the other end of town of just over two square miles were talking about it. That wasn't necessarily a bad thing. Knowing each other could also be advantageous during certain times of the year. On Halloween night, costumed kiddies would bring home large bags filled with homemade treats such as caramel apples or monster cookies. Parents rarely fretted over the thought of unwrapped treats because they sensed who likely passed them out. And when the children rummaged through their trick or treat bag the next day, they probably found fewer contents and crumbs on the kitchen table next to a coffee cup. Or when someone went on a trip, a neighbor would keep a watchful eye on that property, whether asked or not.

Tracy is nestled in the southwest portion of the state, just seven miles west of Walnut Grove, a small community famous for being the home of Laura Ingalls Wilder. But if residents wanted to enjoy life in the big city on occasion, Tracy is also situated only 127 miles southwest of Minneapolis and seventy-one miles northeast of Sioux Falls, the biggest cities in Minnesota and South Dakota, respectively.

Initially called Summit, Tracy later selected the name of a village established in 1870 in honor of John F. Tracy, a railroad officer. It was common in those days to name villages after someone in the railroad company. John F. Tracy was once the president of the Chicago, Rock Island and Pacific Railroad that served as Abraham Lincoln's funeral train as he traveled from Washington, D.C., to his hometown of Springfield, Illinois, for interment. Tracy discontinued its village format and registered as a city under the same name in 1876, three years before the railroad lines would be laid there. As the lines expanded west and south, Tracy soon became the biggest town in the region. Although never mentioned by name, Tracy was referred to in Wilder's book *By the Shores of Silver Lake*, describing the first train ride she took there from Walnut Grove. Tracy was also described as a rail center in Wilder's *The Long Winter*. The Chicago, Rock Island and Pacific Railroad eventually became the Chicago and Northwestern Railway.

Tracy's railroad industry had declined slightly in the late 1960s due to the advent of diesel-powered locomotives and the rise of the trucking industry. The Chicago and Northwestern railroad yard employed approximately twenty-five workers from engineers, conductors, brakemen, and yard workers in the late '60s. Despite the recent hardship, the railroad was still a vital cog in Tracy's economic wheel. To further associate the town's trademark with the railroad industry, Tracy's amateur baseball team was nicknamed the Engineers. And the town's celebration each Labor Day weekend became known as Box Car Days.

Farming was also a powerful industry during this time in Lyon County, as well as surrounding counties. Implement dealers, co-ops and feed salesmen were benefiting from the rich farmland and the area's abundant grain farmers.

Other businesses in town were also prospering during this era as evidenced by six gas stations, five clothing stores, four car dealerships, three grocery stores, three banks, three variety stores, three hardware stores, two drug stores, two furniture stores, two funeral homes and two lumber yards—all numbers representing a steady economy for a community of this size. There were also numerous other businesses, including the 7-Up Bottling Company that had been in operation in Tracy since the early 1900s. And the town also sported six churches.

A majority of the businesses in Tracy had been in operation for many years. Several were second- or third-generation establishments and familiarity in town was as common as humidity and mosquitoes in the summer. Store owners knew nearly every customer by name and often greeted each one as the bell rang on his/her door to indicate a patron was entering. Customers also knew what items each store owner stocked and, if the store did not carry the item desired, the owner would try his best to order it. Carry-out boys at the grocery stores often knew which car the customer was driving and whether they liked bags in the backseat or trunk. So shoppers would stay and chat with the store owners while their goods were being tucked away for the ride home.

Gasoline was only twenty-nine cents per gallon, and attendants would pump the gas and also provide a complimentary oil check and windshield cleaning.

The city's Central Park was seemingly filled by people of all ages whenever weather permitted.

Along with playground equipment of that era spread throughout the picturesque park, there was a baseball field on the north end that transformed into a hockey rink with a warming house in the winter. And there was a tennis and basketball court in the midst of the park. A concrete band shelter used by the school band or a local ensemble to entertain the townspeople on a summer evening stood on the south end of the park.

Just across the street to the west was the Tracy Nursing Home. Residents there often sat outside on lawn chairs or benches and reminisced about the time they had once spent in the park as they listened and watched the activities of the moment. The nursing home was once the town's hospital until a new facility was built southeast of town in 1961.

Tracy wasn't the most exciting town in Minnesota. But there were enough things to do to fend off boredom.

A man-made lake was just a mile north of town near the airport that had been stocked by the Department of Natural Resources with several species of fish. Young angling enthusiasts would spend an evening searching for night crawlers with a flashlight and an old coffee can filled with dirt in anticipation of the next day's excursion to Swift Lake. The pedal-powered trip to the lake felt like going on a vacation. The wire baskets hanging on the sides of a kid's bike, indicating the child also delivered the *Minneapolis Star* newspaper, were often filled with a tackle box, worms, and a sack lunch. Even though the journey took less than ten minutes — longer if bucking the wind — it felt like the city was a hundred miles away closer to the destination. Once there, the rocky shoreline became a kid's second home. If the fish weren't biting, one could watch small planes land or takeoff with the airport just a few hundred yards north of the lake. If lucky enough to land a few lunkers, those same kids could plop the fish in their baskets and lug them back home as quickly as possible.

There was also a nine-hole golf course two miles east of town on Highway 14 where golf balls would go to die. Duffers pretty much knew everyone's handicap, what time they liked to tee off and how fast they played. This was especially advantageous in avoiding slower players. When the course was closed, scavengers could be seen in nearby fields, in the long grass or in creeks scrounging up wayward golf balls. Finding golf balls would stave off the purchase of new ones and friends often competed to see who could find the most.

The Tracy Lanes bowling alley featured six lanes for recreational or league bowling. Teens battling boredom or looking for a place to hang out with friends would often be found at the bowling alley or at Chuck's A&W along Highway 14.

There was also a community swimming pool in town, complete with a high and low board, and a kiddy pool next to it. The high board felt like a plunge from the roof of a skyscraper to beginning swimmers. To those more experienced pool patrons, it was a place to display diving talents. Lifeguards spent their days basking in

the sun and blowing their whistle after catching an exu-
berant youth running along the side of the pool. Rarely
did anyone ever get to see a lifeguard's hair get wet. And
it was forbidden, at least in a child's mind, to leave the
pool without plopping some money down on the
counter for candy or flavored ice treats. For some reason,
a frozen Milky Way or Sugar Daddy sucker tasted better
with wet, wrinkled fingers.

The Hollywood Theatre stood in the middle of
the business district on Third Street. Rarely was it not
filled with moviegoers since there were no VCRs,
DVDs, HBO, or any television channels that showed
current movies during that era. The 425-seat theatre
was regarded as one of the best in the region. Second-
generation theater owner Johnny Glaser often beat
neighboring towns in terms of obtaining current re-
leases. He would show two nightly movies seven days
a week, including two matinees on Sunday. Often he
would show westerns on the weekends. The cost was
one dollar for adults and fifty cents for children. There
were also free movies for the kids during the Christmas
break. Someone dressed as Santa Claus, oftentimes
Glaser himself, would walk up and down the aisles before the movie started to pass out complimentary
candy canes. Glaser, who ran the theater from 1957 to
1978, took tickets himself and greeted people by name.
If a child was at the concession stand and had no
money, Glaser made it a point to make sure that child
had something to munch on during the movie. Sometimes there would be a Midnight Madness, when

viewers could watch movies late at night. On New Year's Eve, he would walk to the front of the theatre and lead patrons in a midnight countdown to the new year. Glaser would pay children fifteen cents each to help pick up popcorn boxes and other garbage in the aisles the morning after a movie.

Another popular spot in town was along U.S. Highway 14 running east and west through town. Edith Revard was the proprietor of a popular popcorn stand, which also served as one of the first drive-through establishments in the region. The red and white building was not much bigger than an ice fishing shanty, but the elderly woman placed it on the edge of her property along the highway so customers traveling from west to east could pull their vehicle over to the shoulder next to her shanty, roll down the window and place their order. A small bag of the buttered popcorn was ten cents. A large bag was twenty-five cents. A breezy day provided Edith with free advertising as the smell of fresh popcorn could be sensed for several blocks.

About the biggest thing to hit Tracy each year was Box Car Days. The three-day extravaganza included a parade, carnival, various games, contest and events, and a Miss Tracy pageant. Glaser often emceed the pageant and became known as Tracy's version of Bert Parks.

And there was the usual sprinkling of ballparks throughout town, although there were just as many games being played in backyards as there were on the diamonds. Rocks, shingles, hubcaps, or cardboard scraps often served as the bases. Every now and then a neighbor's window could be heard shattering, but neighbors rarely were upset about it and would have it fixed by the next day or two. Of course, that was after some kid's father had to fork over the cash.

The high school located between the city park and the business district was thirty-two years old and the elementary school a few blocks to the northwest was seventy years old. A new high school a half-mile south of town was in the infant stages of construction and upon completion, the plan was for the elementary school to close and the younger students to shift over to the old high school.

Tracy was an obscure place. Residents were patient, relaxed and happy for the most part. There were no stoplights to anguish over, nor any parking meters to worry about. The word stress had not manifested into this area yet. Those living outside the region were not familiar with Tracy's whereabouts unless they had to travel there to visit a relative or to attend a sporting event. The town was really not famous for anything. There was no statue to represent a historical figure that had once resided here. There were no astronauts, actors, professional athletes, inventors, musicians, or even a famous outlaw who once resided in this city. About the most exciting thing to occur was in 1927 when a train carrying President Calvin Coolidge and his wife, Grace, on their way to the Black Hills in South Dakota for a vacation made a twenty-minute stop in Tracy.

Then, just as summer was in its infant stages in 1968, Tracy suddenly sprouted fame and became one of the most talked about towns in the state. But the sudden popularity was for all the wrong reasons. Tracy was hit by the first-ever recorded F5 tornado in Minnesota history. The tornado churned through the heart of town in less than ten minutes, rendering it virtually helpless. It wasn't a nuclear bomb that blew twenty-five percent of the town to smithereens. Nor was it a volcano or an earthquake. Anyone could understand how those types of natural disasters were capable of demolishing a town. But it was hard for the town to accept being destroyed this much by wind.

Chapter 4
SOUND THE ALARM

June 13, 1968

THE NATIONAL WEATHER SERVICE'S forecast for June 13 called for the possibility of severe thunderstorms developing in southwestern Minnesota by late afternoon.

The temperature at noon in Tracy had already reached ninety-two degrees and the high humidity made it feel even hotter than that. It was the type of a day best suited for relaxing in the shade, turning the sprinkler on for the kids and making a big pitcher of lemonade. The lawnmower wasn't going anywhere so it might as well just stay parked in the back of the garage. Many people venturing outside sat on their front porch or under a tree to take advantage of the shade, even if it was only a degree or two cooler. Despite limited movement on this "lazy" day, beads of perspiration were still visible on everyone's face. Shirts darkened with perspiration were prevalent. Many townspeople were listening to the Minnesota Twins' baseball game on WCCO radio that afternoon.

The broadcast of the game was often interrupted with updated weather reports. Early in the game, the reports advised elderly people and children to stay indoors and find a way to keep cool since the suffocating humidity would likely affect them the most. By the middle innings of the baseball game, the weather updates on the radio focused more on the impending thunderstorms that were building momentum in South Dakota and heading in an easterly direction toward Minnesota. The National Weather Service in Minneapolis issued severe thunderstorm watches for those areas at 1:10 p.m.

Throughout the day in Tracy, children were playing in sprinklers or were at the city swimming pool in an attempt to combat the heat. Tracy's Central Park was also filled with people on benches, picnic tables or folding chairs; the majority of them trying to take advantage of the abundance of shade. Many were fanning themselves with anything they could find . . . their hand, a hat, or a newspaper provided temporary relief. Most homeowners in the region weren't fortunate enough to own air conditioning and had to produce their own way of staying cool indoors. Sitting in front of a two-foot by two-foot box fan, common in those days, while wetting your face and body with a cloth was a popular choice. Some would even continually open the refrigerator door and stick their head in for a brief sense of relief. Sleeping was difficult on days like this, but occasionally the humidity sapped so much of energy that exhaustion provided an outlet.

Children attempting to sell lemonade from stands constructed from a card table struggled to keep the beverage cool and eventually succumbed to the exhaustion of having to run in and out of their house for ice.

Conversations between neighbors were generally about the weather, most notably the last time anyone could remember it being this hot and humid. Some were still talking about the recent deaths of Robert F. Kennedy, who died exactly a week earlier on June 6 after being shot in Los Angeles, or the slaying of Dr. Martin Luther King two months earlier in Memphis. Others were talking about the Vietnam War or politics. Lyndon Johnson was president, but he had indicated he would not seek re-election. That left vice-president and former Minnesota Senator Hubert H. Humphrey and current Minnesota Senator Eugene McCarthy to battle it out for the Democratic nomination. Richard Nixon was comfortably ahead of Nelson Rockefeller in the race for the Republican nomination.

At 1:30 p.m., Lyon County, where Tracy is situated, was included among several counties placed in a severe thunderstorm watch area until 7:00 p.m. Despite the announcement, citizens weren't scurrying to get home. Rather, most acted as if they weren't all that concerned. The sun was still bearing down upon the city with little cloud relief in sight. While there was only a slight breeze in the morning, the winds were starting to pick up in the afternoon. Still, the extra wind velocity wasn't providing any additional comfort. The thunderstorm watch area called for the possible development of damaging winds, large hail, and dangerous cloud-to-ground lightning strikes. Cities mentioned in the watch area included Tracy, Marshall, and Redwood Falls in southwestern Minnesota and Willmar, St. Cloud, and Alexandria in the west central and central part of the state.

At 2:25 p.m., the temperature was ninety-six degrees, and the National Weather Service personnel in Minneapolis were closely monitoring the development of supercells in eastern parts of South Dakota. They issued a severe thunderstorm warning, as well as a tornado watch, at that time. The watch was issued for most of western Minnesota and was in effect from 4:00 p.m. to 10:00 p.m. Five minutes later, a second severe thunderstorm warning and tornado watch was issued for most of southern Minnesota that would also be in effect from 4:00 p.m. to 10:00 p.m.

June is the month of greatest frequency of tornadoes in Minnesota, which lies along the north edge of the region of maximum occurrences in the United States, commonly known as the Tornado Belt. Of all the recorded tornadoes that touched the ground in Minnesota history, thirty-seven percent have occurred in June. July is next at twenty-five percent. And most tornadoes in Minnesota have touched down between 2:00 p.m. and 9:00 p.m., but have been recorded at any time of day or night.

It became commonplace in southwest Minnesota to see funnels churning among the clouds at least a couple of times in the summer during a sultry stretch. Usually, they danced overhead and occasionally dipped down a little as if teasing people, but they rarely two-stepped to the ground, save for a few times in the country where only some crops or an occasional silo or barn suffered damage. Not since June 9, 1947, had a tornado come even close to Tracy. That twister caused only moderate damage to a few farms sites. A tornado on June 22, 1924, also touched down four miles south of town, killing one man, John Edwards. That twister dissipated before reaching city limits.

The heaviest storm activity by 3:30 p.m. was occurring near the South Dakota/Minnesota border, approximately fifty miles from Tracy. Strong winds were felling trees and power lines in the extreme eastern parts of South Dakota. Frequent lightning strikes were also knocking out power to that area.

Newspaper carriers delivering the *Minneapolis Tribune*, an afternoon paper at the time, were perspiring heavily from lugging the weighted canvas bag over one shoulder. They weren't allowed to toss the paper on the front lawn as in years past, so the job of having to walk to each customer's door made it more grueling. Especially when the temperature was higher than most of the paperboys' weight.

The Twins were now wrapping up a 3 to 1 loss to the Detroit Tigers and eventual Cy Young Award winner Denny McLain at Tiger Stadium. Residents of Tracy who listened to the radio or watched television heard about the severe weather now heading their way. News of this sort traveled throughout the small community like a prairie fire in high winds. But the report was a welcome announcement to many. With rain headed their way, the citizens anticipated relief from the sultry day. But this storm wasn't about to give anyone any type of relief, and Tracy was in the direct line of fire.

Just after 5:00 p.m., the southwestern portion of the sky from Tracy's vantage point was still virtually cloudless. Some rain clouds were visible in the western sky, but nothing appeared to be too threatening. Bill Bolin, a high school history teacher and also the coach of Tracy's American Legion baseball team, checked the weather reports, saw that it didn't appear to be any threat to the area at this time and gave the "thumbs up" for bus driver Warner "Fritz" Lessman to transport the team to Cottonwood, a town fifteen miles north of Tracy, for a scheduled 6:30 p.m. start time.

Soon after the bus carrying the baseball team left Tracy, the National Weather Service's radar was indicating that a new wave of storms were intensifying just a few miles over the Minnesota border or forty-five miles to the west of Tracy. The sky there was virtually exploding with activity, and National Weather Service personnel were attempting to monitor the activity and relay the latest developments as quickly as they could.

Reports began filing into media outlets from various locations that damaging hail—some stones as large as tennis balls—were accompanied by dangerous and frequent cloud-to-ground lightning strikes with winds in excess of seventy-five miles per hour in extreme southern and southwestern Minnesota.

People living in the watch area were advised to be prepared to seek shelter and stay away from power lines and windows if threatening weather approached their area. The large hail that fell over parts of those areas damaged hundreds of automobiles, broke windows in at least twenty-five homes and businesses, and leveled crops. Two men received minor injuries when struck by hail in Pipestone County, forty-five miles southwest of Tracy.

Upon hearing this latest report about severe weather approaching from the southwest, Tracy citizens looked skyward. But the sun's brightness and the blue sky with small splashes of wispy light-gray and white clouds fooled them. Shrugging their shoulders, many of the onlookers figured the report was either inaccurate or those responsible for including Tracy in the watch area had been in the heat too long. A closer inspection would have revealed a menacing-looking wall cloud forming along the base of a cumulonimbus cloud in the lower southwestern sky.

Just as the Tracy baseball team arrived in Cottonwood around 5:45 p.m., rain started to fall. As the bus pulled into the ballpark, it became a torrential downpour. Unsure if they would get precipitation in Cottonwood that day, field workers had just finished spraying the diamond with water as was the norm on dry summer days to keep the dust to a minimum while the game was being played. With lightning also visible nearby and the forecast calling for severe weather, Bolin and Cottonwood coach Bob Jaeger agreed with the two umpires that the game should be postponed. The fourteen Tracy players re-boarded the bus, and Lessman began the journey back home.

The rain stopped shortly after the Tracy squad left Cottonwood on Highway 19. The rain clouds moved northeast, and the rest of sky was relatively clear albeit for a charcoal-colored thunderhead looming in the southwest horizon. From Highway 19, Lessman turned the bus south onto County Road 11, also called the Airport Road, and began to drive the school bus the final fifteen miles straight south into Tracy.

Around 6:00 p.m., Delpha Koch was inside her home preparing the evening meal on a farm one mile east of Garvin and four miles southwest of Tracy. Delpha's sons, Allan, who had just graduated from Tracy High School a few weeks earlier, and Bruce, who had just completed eighth grade, had finished their chores and entered the house. Delpha's husband, Melvin, was working in the field on his grain and livestock farm.

Like a shark looking for prey, the threatening weather was now heading toward Tracy and approaching the vicinity of the Koch's farm. At 6:45 p.m., the National Weather Service in Kansas City, Missouri, replaced the two previous National Weather Service tornado watches issued by the Minneapolis bureau with a new one until 1:00 a.m. The watch area resembled a capital "L," covering most of western and southern Minnesota. Tornadoes were likely to hit somewhere in this area, meteorologists figured. It was just a matter of where and how many.

Melvin was wrapping up work for the day and was heading for home on his tractor when he noticed a wall cloud expanding and looking nastier by the minute. He was especially curious about what he thought was rotation. So he stopped the tractor to have a closer look and noticed a funnel shape starting to emerge. He had seen rotating clouds form funnel shapes many times before out in the country, but none of them had ever touched the ground. He usually watched as they would quietly dissipate or return to the wall cloud as if it was the mother ship calling them home. Melvin continued toward home on the tractor, while continuing to watch the funnel's tail. It was now protruding further from the wall cloud than others he had witnessed before. The rotation was well east of their farm place so Melvin figured the farm wasn't in harm's way. But he was certain other farm places wouldn't be as fortunate if the funnel touched ground and formed a tornado.

Just as he stopped the tractor next to the barn, he noticed dirt and debris on the ground below the funnel starting to kick up and fly around. He jumped down off the tractor and went into the house as quickly as he could to inform Delpha, who was a nurse at the Tracy Hospital, what he had just seen approaching. The funnel had touched down, and the tornado was making its way in the direction of Tracy. After Delpha stepped outside and saw the powerful rotation, she agreed with Melvin that a call needed to be placed to warn the citizens of Tracy. Allan and Bruce also watched as the tornado headed toward Tracy. The family farm was built on a knoll, which afforded them a clear view of inclement weather.

Delpha went back into the house, grabbed the receiver from the rotary-dial wall phone in the kitchen and dialed the numbers 6-2-9-5-5-3-4 for the Tracy police department. When dispatcher Julius DeBlieck took the call from Delpha, it was 6:53 p.m. As a critical condition nurse, Delpha knew how important it was to remain calm when relaying information. She informed the dispatcher of the location that she had spotted the tornado and that it was now crossing Highway 59 and heading straight for Tracy. With tornadoes traveling an average of thirty miles per hour and this one four miles from town when he took the call, Julius figured the town would be hit within ten minutes.

DeBlieck knew that he needed to verify the information he had just received before pulling the switch to activate the civil defense alarm. The dispatcher's office in Tracy had received tornado reports in the past that turned out to be nothing more than a band of tail clouds that often attached to a wall cloud and resembled a funnel. He also had received phony calls a few times from pranksters hoping to dupe him into sounding the siren. DeBlieck didn't want the townspeople to panic if it wasn't necessary. But he also knew he needed to react quickly, and he had known the Kochs for years so he set off the warning siren at 6:55 p.m. Other concerned farmers called in to the dispatcher soon after Delpha, so Julius knew he did the right thing by sounding the alarm.

Bernie Holm, who wore more hats in town than a haberdashery store model, was sitting at his kitchen table with his wife, Netter. Their fifteen-year-old daughter, Marsha, was getting ready to participate in a scheduled band concert at the city park. Bernie had decided to "grab a quick bite to eat" before heading out to the Tracy Municipal Cemetery one mile south of town to water the plants and flowers in the huge urns scattered around the grounds. Bernie and Netter had owned the Tracy Greenhouse along Highway 14 since 1949. The greenhouse sat just across the highway from their home on Third Street. Bernie was also Tracy's fire marshall, fire chief, and Civil Defense director. And, when needed, he would help out at the cemetery because of his green thumb. "Bernie" and "idleness" was not often used in the same sentence.

While eating his sandwich, Holm peered out the window and noticed what he described as "white crickets" in his front lawn. In actuality, it had begun raining and hailing, and the stones were bouncing off the grass like crickets on a drought-stricken prairie. Housewives could be seen all over town scurrying outside to bring in their laundry from the clothesline and also to inform their children playing in the yard to come inside the house. Hail the size of peas were soon bouncing off the roads like ping pong balls.

Chomping on his last bite of food, Bernie headed out the door to look at the weather. Before he closed the door behind him, the phone rang. Marsha picked up the receiver. It was Julius relaying the information that a tornado was reportedly approaching from the southwest. Bernie had a feeling that this report was no prank because of the rain and hail that often preceded a tornado. Before he got into his car, Bernie turned to Netter, who was standing at the front door observing the weather, and told her to take Marsha and the family dog and go down into the basement and stay there until he came back home.

The protocol in the dispatcher's office was that if a fire was reported, Julius would use a red phone that would simultaneously ring at the fire chief's home, as well as the homes of nine other firemen. Generally, after receiving the call, firemen would rush to the firehouse. The wives of those ten firemen would then each dial a predetermined number of other firemans' homes. That way, twenty firemen were put on notice. Not all firemen were home to take the call so the fire whistle on the civil defense system's pole on the north side of town or the siren located on top of the municipal building would also help page the crew. This time, Julius used the red fire phone when calling Bernie about this reported tornado sighting so other firemen could also be alerted.

Bernie was formerly the town's mayor in 1961. One of his first duties was to try to fill the request of many residents and purchase a second civil defense system. Since the town lay in the tornado belt, citizens felt that one day the lack of adequate warning sirens could prove costly. The city had one siren atop the municipal building, but some citizens north of Highway 14 couldn't hear it. Tests done by the civil defense department indicated that homes in that area were as much as 200 feet lower in elevation than the business district where the municipal building was located. That led to the discovery that the siren's wail was carrying over the top of the houses north of town. The city council agreed that there was a need for a second warning siren and gave Bernie authority to search for a more modern system. He made several calls to companies that sold the siren systems and also contacted other civil defense directors in other towns inquiring which system would be the best fit for Tracy. The city council voted in favor of the city granting a portion of the money for the project. The state civil defense department matched the funds.

When the new siren was purchased, it was mounted atop the municipal building because it had a wider range and the old siren was taken down and erected close to Highway 14.

The steady wail of the siren meant a tornado was spotted nearing the city limits. A wavering up-and-down siren, distinctly different than the one used to indicate a tornado or other natural disaster, was used for a fire. The town's civil defense warning system also included a siren in case of an air raid that Holm described as a "bellering cow." Tracy was one of the first cities in the region to have a three-signal system.

To make certain citizens became accustomed to the tone for a tornado, Tracy's civil defense team blew the whistle on the first Wednesday of each month. There was no "all-clear" signal available on this particular model.

After receiving the call from Julius, Bernie sped off in his car and headed to the police station in the municipal building six blocks south. The fire station was also housed in that building. Bernie arrived in less than one minute, slamming on the brakes in front of the building. After coming to a screeching halt, he hopped out as quickly as he could and raced up the sidewalk leading to the front door of the municipal building. Other firemen who received the phone call from Julius, were arriving simultaneously and also running to the door.

By now the sky was turning an eerie shade of green. Longtime residents of Tracy said they had never seen the sky that color before. The rain kept coming down, had become vicious, and the wind was gusting to thirty-five miles per hour. The hail was also increasing in size, and the green lawns looked like a driving range after a busy day at the golf course.

According to numerous eyewitness accounts, the tornado formed near Lake Sarah, which lay approximately twelve miles southwest of the city limits of Tracy by air. Although various birth times were given for the funnel from eyewitnesses at or near Lake Sarah, likely because it had dipped several times from the wall cloud before eventually touching down, the National Weather Service declared the time as 6:48 p.m. Many of those who first saw the tornado were in agreement that it wouldn't stay on the ground long enough to reach Tracy.

The radar in Minneapolis picked up the tornado southwest of Tracy and estimated it was traveling around thirty to thirty-five miles per hour and moving in a northeasterly direction. It was also estimated that initial wind speeds when the tornado first touched down were just over 125 miles per hour.

Police officer Strann Nelson, in a modern-day version of Paul Revere, had spotted the tornado while on duty and drove the squad car up and down several streets of Tracy with the siren blasting, warning residents on his public address system to get to a safe place immediately.

Once inside the dispatcher's office, Bernie located Julius and asked him where the tornado was now located. The two men looked out the front window and saw the tornado, now ghostly white, churning on the outskirts of town. Bernie told Julius to set the second cycle of the siren on manual and to find a place of safety. Bernie also told the other firemen at the station to take cover as quickly as possible. Julius headed into the municipal building's basement, followed by a few of the firemen who didn't want to risk driving home.

Bernie ran back outside and got in his car, driving over sixty miles per hour on residential streets while heading north to his home. With his thought process all discombobulated from the excitement of the moment, Bernie worried about getting a speeding ticket and not being able to get home to check on his family. Bernie slammed on the car's brakes in front of his house and his civic pride came into play once more when thought he might be ticketed for illegally parking on the wrong side of the street in front of his house. As he burst through the front door, the kitchen windows began to shatter, and Bernie shouted for his family to get into the basement, forgetting he had told them earlier to seek shelter. Netter, Marsha, and the family dog already huddled in the basement and Bernie shielded them as much as possible.

Chapter 5
A FAMILY GATHERING

June 13, 1968

O
N THE MORNING OF JUNE 13, Linda and Nancy awoke around 7:00 a.m. Neither of them were able to sleep comfortably with the heat and high humidity turning the small house into a sauna. Linda positioned the box fan so the air stream would reach the kitchen table. She then set Nancy down in the high chair and prepared a bowl of cereal and a cup of apple juice for the little girl. Linda had toast to go with her orange juice. Nancy wasn't in her usual pleasant mood, and Linda figured it was because of a small rash that had developed around her mouth. The rash was obviously irritating Nancy, who continually put her hands on it in an attempt to alleviate the itching. So Linda made an appointment with Dr. Norman Lee, one of two physicians in town. Dr. Lee had an opening for 1:30 p.m. that day and told Linda to give Nancy a couple of baby aspirins to help ease her discomfort until then.

After finishing breakfast, Linda put the dishes in the sink and then began getting Nancy dressed for the day. She picked out a pink shorts outfit with white lace around the edges of the shorts and the shirt sleeves. She then slipped on her white shoes, leaving off the socks because of the heat. She next brushed Nancy's hair. Nancy had smooth sandy-colored hair that hung just over her ears and straight bangs just above her eyebrows. Her eyes were bright blue and her cheeks were plump and rosy red.

As she often did, Linda would make the short drive to her mother's place this morning for a visit and let her siblings play with Nancy and possibly keep the child's mind off the rash until the appointment to see the doctor. As soon as Linda stepped outside the front door of her home with Nancy in her arms, a blanket of mugginess smothered them. It was hard to even take a deep breath.

Harriet Timmerman, who lived next door to Linda with her husband, Rodney, was outside hanging clothes on the line. Linda and Harriet spoke briefly about the four mongrel puppies Linda had in a pen behind a shed on her rental property. Linda asked Harriet if the six-week-old puppies' yelping was annoying, and Harriet assured her that they were no bother. Lady, the mother to the puppies, had been run over by a school bus three weeks earlier, so Linda had taken over care of the puppies.

Linda placed Nancy in the Thunderbird and drove to her mother's house in a section of town known as Broadacres, which was also on the southern fringe of Tracy and nearly one mile east of the Greenwood section. Three of Linda's four younger sisters,

Pam, eight; Georgia, six; and Abbie, five, were home with their mother. Kathy, nineteen and only eleven months younger than Linda, was married and living in Storden, twenty-eight miles southeast of Tracy. Linda's only brother, Charles, seventeen, was working at Lindy's Repair, owned by his father, Clarence. The "Lindy" moniker came about since Clarence's middle name was Lindbergh, which his parents decided since he was born on July 26, 1927, two months after Charles A. Lindbergh became the first aviator to make a solo transatlantic flight. Charles, always known as Chuck to his family and friends, and Linda's names were derivations of Lindbergh.

When Linda pulled the Thunderbird into her mother's gravel driveway, the three siblings were already outside playing and all came running up to the car to see Nancy. The sisters mockingly fought over who would get to carry Nancy first, each gently pulling on an arm or a leg, which normally made the little girl giggle. But Nancy was morose throughout the day, as were most people due to the intense heat and humidity. The girls stayed outdoors and played, while Linda talked inside the house with her mother. Betty was planning to make a hot dish for dinner and asked Linda and Nancy to stay and eat with them.

After dinner, Linda took Nancy to her appointment at the clinic, located in the business district of town. Dr. Lee examined Nancy for a few minutes, determined the rash was not serious or contagious, then scrawled down a prescription on a notepad that he felt would alleviate the problem in a few days. Nancy was generally shy and took several meetings with someone before she got over her uneasiness. In Dr. Lee's office, the little girl fidgeted and squealed each time the doctor examined her ears or mouth. One of Dr. Lee's nurses gave Nancy a lollipop before they left and told Linda to call if the rash persisted.

Even though Linda was in the doctor's office only a short while, the wave of heat she felt when opening the car door was similar to standing too close to a oven when the door is first opened to check on the contents. This was the type of day that sapped the energy out of the young and old alike.

Linda returned to her mother's house for a short while to tell her what the doctor had said about Nancy's rash. Before returning to her home in Greenwood, Linda decided she would first go into town and stop at John's Rx Drug on Third Street to fill the prescription Dr. Lee had written out for Nancy. Generally, if one of Linda's siblings wanted to come home with her and help take care of Nancy, the others would also want to go. On this day, though, only Pam decided to go with Linda and stay overnight.

As the family stood outside saying goodbye to one another shortly after 5:00 p.m., Bill Hall, an elderly bachelor who lived next door to Betty, came outside and informed the girls that Tracy was in a severe thunderstorm watch and that Linda should stay at her mother's house. When he pointed toward the southwest portion of the sky while telling that a storm was soon expected to be rearing its ugly thunderhead, the girls all looked in that direction, but none seemed particularly concerned about his forecast. As if taking a page out of the *Farmer's Almanac*, the bachelor prognosticated that there would be an abundance of inclement weather in Tracy this summer. This impending storm, he went on, was going to be severe and persisted in his concern that Linda should stay where she was. But Linda, who seemingly always turned a deaf ear when a conversation was about storms, wanted to get the prescription for Nancy and then go home and relax. She politely thanked Hall for his concern and assured him that she would be fine. The only thought she had concerning the weather was that, if it rained, the town might get a splash of relief from the heat.

Pam sat in the front passenger seat, while Nancy stood between them. Nancy enjoyed riding in a car and rarely sat down because she was too short to see out the windows. Linda was so used to the little girl standing next to her in the car that her right arm automatically extended across Nancy's chest like a barricade when the brakes were applied. Linda drove downtown and parked in front of John's Drug. The three girls got out of the vehicle and went into the store around 5:30 p.m. The bells signifying a customer had come through the front door startled Nancy. John Schleppenbach, an outgoing and personable pharmacist who owned the establishment, always greeted his customers with a loud and cheerful voice that would reverberate throughout the store. Linda handed him the prescription. After perusing the doctor's scrawls on the paper, Schleppenbach looked at the rash around Nancy's mouth, talked to her for a moment and then took her hands and clapped them together in a playful manner. The girl clung to Linda's leg as the druggist proceeded to fill the prescription.

The wait was brief as Schleppenbach soon came out from behind the counter with the medicine. He briefly tried to get Nancy to smile again, but to no avail. Then he asked Linda if she knew a storm was possibly heading toward Tracy. She told Schleppenbach that she was aware of the threat of bad weather. He then thanked her for coming in, while following the three girls to the front door. As they got into the car, Linda could see Schleppenbach checking out the sky.

Once in the sauna-like car, Linda told Pam that she couldn't wait to get home so they could sit in front of one of the several fans stationed in rooms inside the house. By now, the dark wall cloud in the southwest sky had almost doubled in size from when Bill Hall pointed it out. But Linda still paid no attention with the rest of the sky still blue.

When she arrived home, Linda read the instructions on the medicine bottle. Nancy squawked every time Linda pushed the spoon toward her mouth, turning her head back and forth in an attempt to keep her mouth as far away as possible. After a few attempts, Linda finally managed to get Nancy to swallow the medicine, followed by a dramatic face contortion as if the little girl had just tasted something rotten. Pam then kept Nancy entertained as best she could while Linda went outside to feed the puppies. With Clifford away, Linda's family members often provided companionship and assistance for her and Nancy. The puppies, in a sheltered pen, were excited to see Linda bringing them food. They climbed on each other's backs in an attempt to get to the food via any route they could. There were two female and two male puppies. One male was nearly all white, save for a dark spot here and there. The other three were mostly black and brown with a few dabs of white.

It was now starting to rain, so Linda rolled up the windows in the car parked in the front of the house. She even paused for a moment while closing her eyes and tilting her head upwards to allow the refreshing drops to splash on her face. The slight breeze cooled the wetness on her arms and face and brought about a sense of comfort for the first time on this day. As she opened her eyes, she saw the storm cloud. It was dark and nasty looking, but still held no special meaning to her other than rain, lightning, and thunder. She had never been in any kind of dangerous weather and never remembered having to seek shelter in a basement. She had learned years earlier that if a dangerous thunderstorm or even a tornado was approaching, she should go into the southwest corner of the basement.

Linda realized it was much too hot to make anything on the stove or in the oven for supper.

Besides, the girls didn't have much of an appetite in this type of weather. So Linda just made peanut butter and jelly sandwiches. Pam helped put Nancy in her high chair. Linda was like a second mother to Pam, who always felt comfortable at her big sister's home. After the girls finished eating, Linda laid an exhausted Nancy down in her crib on the north side of the house for a nap.

As she was preparing to wash dishes, Linda removed her class ring from her finger and set it on the kitchen window sill as she always did. As she began washing and placing the dishes in the rack, Pam dried them and put each one away in the cupboards. When they were finished, Linda decided to write her daily letter to Clifford in the service in Washington. Linda rarely missed a day writing to Clifford, knowing he would appreciate getting mail and being informed of what was going on back home. And Clifford almost always reciprocated with a letter to her as well. Linda checked on Nancy, who was fast asleep, then walked quietly back into the kitchen. Linda took a pen, some manila school paper and an envelope from a drawer in the kitchen, then sat down at the kitchen table.

Pam sat on top of the table and offered Linda several bits of information that could be included in the letter. The rain was falling harder now.

Linda began this letter like every one she wrote her husband:

Cliffy.

Chapter 6

GREENWOOD GETS HIT

LINDA EXPRESSED VIRTUALLY NO FEAR when it came to storms. Rarely did she listen to weather reports or even to absorb the neighborhood chatter about severe weather looming whenever dark clouds appeared in the sky. Even when she was a small child, the loud reverberation of thunder didn't intimidate her.

Linda had never witnessed a storm wreaking havoc on a city, nor did she ever expect to. So what if a few branches fell? She didn't feel it was anything to become alarmed about. She always felt safe inside a home or any stable structure. In her mind, rain, hail, and wind was no match for wood or bricks.

Hearing the weather's wrath outside on this Thursday, Linda peered out the front door window from the home she and her husband, Clifford, were renting in Greenwood. She saw the wind forcing the hard rain in a horizontal direction, but just shrugged her shoulders and went back into the kitchen to sit down. She actually felt a sense of calm when it came to storms. And when it rained at night, the incessant *pitter-patter* on the roof often made her sleep better.

Unbeknownst to Linda and Pam, the tornado that had been spotted and reported by the Kochs was now bearing down on the Greenwood section of Tracy like a scud missile, and there was no way to stop it. The only chance the town had of fending off destruction was if the tornado suddenly dissipated. Having traveled nearly twelve miles already, the tornado had progressed into an F5 category with wind in excess of 300 miles per hour. From what started out as less than a block-wide path in the country, the twister had now nearly tripled in size.

As it was getting close to 7:00 p.m., it was becoming increasingly difficult for Pam and Linda to converse, let alone hear the civil defense siren, with the slamming of the rain and hail against the house. Still, Linda wasn't worrying about the potential of severe weather and did not bother to turn on the radio or television to listen to weather reports. But she was becoming nervous about the Thunderbird parked in front of the house. She put down her pen, got up from the table and went to the window to see if the automobile had endured any damage from the hail.

The rain was now coming down so hard that the visibility was similar to a Minnesota blizzard. Despite all the commotion, Nancy remained asleep in her bed, unaware of the events unfolding outside.

Pam pleaded with Linda to let her go outside and pick up some of the large hailstones covering the Vaskes' lawn and bring them in the house. But Linda advised against it, fearing her younger sister would be injured if a hailstone happened to hit her on the head.

After a few minutes of heavy downpour, it suddenly became eerily quiet. The hail stopped, and the rain was limited to just a few scattered drops. The southwest sky had became the color of pea soup. Linda continued writing her letter to Clifford with Pam still sitting on top of the table. While Pam was offering suggestions for the letter, Linda asked her to stop talking for a moment. She thought she heard a siren, either from a police car, fire truck, or an ambulance. As the two listened quietly, Linda figured out that the fire whistle was sounding. Her initial thought was that lightning had probably struck somewhere in town and caused a fire and the city's alarm had been activated.

A few blocks away, Linda and Pam's mother, Betty, was heading to the basement of her home with their sisters Georgia and Abbie and a cousin, Debbie Carlson. Their father and brother were working at the auto repair shop and were closely watching the weather as the warning siren blared. The shop was two blocks north of Betty's house and four blocks east of where Linda lived. They could see the tornado likely would strike Linda's house, while the shop and the Broadacres section were out of the direct path. Chuck wanted to warn Linda of the danger, so he jumped in his 1955 Buick and sped off.

Carson Johnson, who had spotted the tornado from his car window, sped through the streets of

Greenwood with his driver's window down, shouting for people to take cover. Harriet Timmerman was outside and could tell by Carson's voice that something bad was about to happen. So she rushed her children into the basement. Even though they lived only a few feet away from the Timmermans' home, Pam and Linda were unable to hear Carson's warning shouts.

The sisters could now hear a deep rumbling in the distance, similar to a jet taking off, intensifying with each second that passed. The train tracks were north of Linda's house, and she had grown accustomed to the sounds the cars made as they passed by. But she had never heard anything like this and was now becoming increasingly concerned. Linda, with Pam close behind, went to the front door in an attempt to disclose the mystery of what was initiating the unfamiliar sound. The willow tree in the front yard was now bent over in a U-shape and the house was starting to shake from the sudden fury. For the first time in her life, Linda was petrified of what Mother Nature was unfolding. The siblings simultaneously let out a scream.

Linda sternly ordered Pam to get into the basement immediately. Pam didn't recall ever hearing Linda yell at her quite like that and it frightened her even more. Linda scurried into Nancy's bedroom and plucked the little girl out of her bed like a seagull swooping down and nabbing a fish from a water. Pam was aghast with all the commotion going on and, instead of going into the basement as her sister demanded, instead followed her into Nancy's room. Linda, clutching Nancy as tightly as she could to her chest without hurting her, again commanded Pam to get into the basement. Just as they reached the living room en route to the kitchen, all the windows in the house shattered, and the three barefooted girls were showered with glass fragments. Pam then ran as quickly toward the basement door as her trembling legs would allow and was three steps ahead of Linda and Nancy.

The back door, located in the kitchen on the south side of the house, suddenly was ripped from the hinges by the fierce wind. Nancy began to cry uncontrollably as Linda and Pam let out another scream.

The door to the basement was also located in the kitchen, and the girls continued their pursuit to safety. Linda could feel her heart pounding so hard that it felt like it would explode. Pam, shivering with fright, descended three steps to the basement and could go no further against the forces. In a split second, all three girls were blown out the open back door on the south side of the house. Linda, still holding onto Nancy, was hurtled out the door first and slammed to the ground. Pam's head rapped hard against the door frame before she was forced out of the house.

Chuck, unaware of the events unfolding inside Linda's home, could see that he would not be able to make it to her house in time to warn her and instead stayed on the east side of the tornado. He continued driving south until he was behind the twister and could safely park his car. He witnessed the force's initial contact with Greenwood, first tearing apart Ira and Nell Alexander's home located on the extreme southwestern portion. He watched as houses were torn apart with such ease that he could hardly believe it was real. Solid structures flattened in a blink of an eye. It was as if he were at a drive-in movie theater. He was unable to see Linda's house from his vantage point, but knew it was in the direct path, and he began to feel queasy.

As Pam was being swept away three feet above the ground, she saw Linda being blown around on the front lawn. Pam was carried in an upright position for nearly 350 feet to the east and then set down gently on her feet in the front yard of an undamaged home. Although she saw large unidentifiable objects continually whizzing past her while she was airborne, that none of them struck her was inexplicable. She could feel the pelting of sand and dirt against her skin as if she were being stung by a swarm of bees.

Pam had no idea how far she had been carried off. As she was settling to the ground, she noticed a man looking at her through his basement window, then vanish from view as if he were coming out to retrieve her. But in a matter of seconds, the sixty-pound girl was again airborne.

Linda was rolled several yards from the house by the intense wind. With her head slammed repeatedly to the turf, Linda was unable to maintain her hold on the little girl. A large metal object was driven completely through Linda's left calf like a torpedo through water. Several other boards and tree branches also struck her. The top half of the picket fence in her front yard had been busted off, leaving only the bottom portion secured to the ground. Linda was blown over the sharp splintered pieces, which caused a large tear in the top of her right leg. Her right foot became lodged in between two busted pickets. As the foot remained stationary, Linda was tossed from her chest to her back. Her foot was turned 180 degrees, tearing the skin all around the ankle.

The wind continued to bounce Linda on the ground until her foot became dislodged from the fence and she was then blown into the street a few yards from her property. The house she lived in was lifted from its foundation and momentarily hovered above the foundation before being blown apart as if it were filled with dynamite. As the tornado carried the ruins away, Pam was blown back the same way she left, vertically, and set down gently on her feet. When she looked down, her feet were stationed near the front steps where the Vaskes' home once stood.

Chapter 7
OVER THE TRACKS

A S THE FULLY-CHARGED TORNADO bore down on the Greenwood section, Chicago and Northwestern train number 126 with fifty-two cars was nearing the rail yard in Tracy. The train's conductor, Vincent Carey of Tracy, and three crew members from Huron, South Dakota, were aboard. The majority of the box cars were empty, except for three loaded refrigerated cars and four loaded piggy-back cars. The train had coupled in Huron, and Jim Bauman was the engineer. The brakemen were Milton King and Lloyd Melber. During the train's last few miles into Tracy, the rain and hail was coming down so hard that it was almost impossible for the men aboard to see anything outside from the windows of the engine or caboose.

Ted Anderson, Art Goergen, and Frank Greenman were on the yard crew that day and radioed to the number 126 unit that a tornado was heading into town just behind them.

As the engine reached the depot, the rain began to let up, and the crew members could hear the civil defense siren blaring. Carey feared that some of the townspeople would liken it to the fire whistle. So he had Bauman run the train up and down the tracks while sounding the strident diesel horn in hopes that residents would realize there was something much worse than a fire about to hit town.

Neither Linda or Pam had heard the train's whistles five blocks southeast of the depot before the tornado hit Greenwood.

With the relentless beast now bearing down on them, the four men exited the train to seek shelter. But the men had precious seconds and had to settle for the first thing that looked even remotely safe. Goergen hurled himself down the basement stairs and received several cuts and bruises. Anderson crawled under the train's engine. Greenman settled for jumping into a repair shop pit. Carey, scrambling to find someplace to go for safey, ended up diving into a drainage ditch along the tracks. King, who was with Carey in the caboose, ran to a house nearby and was allowed into the residents' basement. Melber was riding in the engine with Bauman and both were well east of the path of the tornado. They crouched beside the engine to protect themselves.

After pummeling the Greenwood area, the vicious vortex marched forward like a football team's fullback lowering his head and hitting the opposing team's defensive line. The twister then rammed its tail into the idle train and derailed twenty-six of the boxcars. One of the empty twenty-five-ton cars was lifted and blown over two blocks away. Two others were rolled over homes like dice in a craps game and came to rest 300 feet away.

Carey was struck by several boards but escaped serious injury. He was also dangerously close to having one of the boxcars fall on him in the ditch. The tornado was initially heading in a northeasterly direction when it reached Tracy, but had its path altered a few degrees toward the north after churning through the boxcars.

The tornado narrowly missed carrying off a full LP gas tank located near the railroad yard, avoiding a possible explosion somewhere in town.

While the majority of the town's people huddled in their basements likened the sound of the tornado overhead to that of a train, several of the train employees said it sounded like a giant vacuum sucking up the town.

About this time, Hollywood Theater owner Johnny Glaser was preparing for the 7:30 p.m. viewing of *Planet of the Apes,* starring Charlton Heston on main street when the tornado was on the outskirts of town. He stepped outside once he saw the rain had let up and began to sweep the sidewalk in front of the theatre. As he opened the front door facing Third Street to the east, he heard the screeching of car tires and then saw several vehicles driving recklessly past his theatre and heading north. Initially, he figured it was "those darn kids" showing off again. But when he looked into the sky, he soon found out why the pedals were to the metal. The tornado was fast approaching and Glaser bolted back inside and ducked under a heavy table in the theatre's basement. He was sure the theater was going to be hit and likely would have had the tornado not been knocked off course after burrowing through the train cars.

By now, the American Legion baseball team was only six miles from Tracy on the Airport Road. Lessman, Bolin, and the players then spotted the tornado, but most thought it was west of town and would not reach the city limits. Rather than continue and risk being caught in the path of the tornado, Lessman stopped the bus about five miles from town. The windows of the bus were filled with faces pressed against them, all watching the "dancing monster" in awe as if they were at a drive-in movie. Because they didn't know the tornado was ripping through town, some of the players joked about it being a "white tornado" like the Ajax liquid cleanser television commercial. Only this white tornado wasn't cleaning up a mess. It was creating one.

Bolin and Lessman feared the worst, having a sense of what was likely happening. They realized the town was indeed in the direct path and that their own families, as well as the families of the boys aboard the bus, might be in peril.

After crossing the railroad tracks, the tornado was now heading toward the center of Tracy. Several of those people living in Greenwood felt safe to crawl out of their basements with the decibel level of the tornado diminishing. Numerous citizens living nearby who had not lost their homes ascended upon the suburban area to help. Linda found herself in the street near the front of her house, dazed and trembling, but feeling none of the affects of her serious injuries. When she first looked around, she thought she was at the city dump as piles of wreckage were on all sides of her. She did not see any sign of Nancy or Pam and knew she had to find them. Despite not being in any shape to stand or walk, Linda managed to pick herself up from the street and even took a few steps before her neighbor Harriet Timmerman, who had been in the basement with her three children, saw her. Linda was bleeding profusely from her head, one arm, both legs, and her ankle. Her fourth toe had been severed and her little toe next to it was barely still attached to her foot. Her entire body was covered with dirt and grime, mixing with the blood to form a dark, sticky paste.

The Timmerman's home had been completely leveled as well, but Harriet had managed to grab a blanket from the basement and rushed to help Linda. Fearing the young woman might go into shock, Harriet wrapped the blanket around Linda. At the same time, Kenny Anderson arrived with his son Danny to check on their friends, the Timmermans. Kenny knew Harriet's husband was working out of town, so he and his son jumped in the car and drove as close as they could get to the damaged area. He was able to park about a block from the Timmermans. He and Danny jumped out of the car and ran over to where the Timmermans' house had once stood. He saw Harriet with her arm around an injured woman and quickly assisted. Linda, who was losing a lot of blood, needed medical attention immediately. With her foot and legs severely injured, Kenny and Danny carried her in a sitting position, using their arms as a makeshift chair — one arm acting as the seat under her thighs and the other arm behind her like a back rest. Although Linda was a willowy woman, it was still difficult for the Andersons to move with any rapidity to their vehicle carrying her in that position.

While being carried Linda continued to call out for Pam and Nancy, still unsure of their status. She still wasn't aware of the extent of her own injuries; her focus being only on the girls.

Pam was standing only fifty yards away, frozen with fear. Her brother had managed to drive his Buick close to where Linda's house had been and didn't notice the two men carrying her away. Nervous and scared, Chuck hopped out of his car and started to look for any sign of Linda, Pam, and Nancy. He figured they had gone into the basement so he figured he would help them out. In all the commotion and with dust hovering over the entire area, Chuck didn't notice Pam as he ran past her. His younger sister then stopped crying and tried to get her brother's. attention. "It's me . . . Pam . . . your little sister," she said, her voice trembling. "Don't you recognize me?"

It was hard for anyone to recognize her. She, too, was bleeding and covered with filth. Chuck turned toward the direction of the voice and was stunned when he saw Pam standing a few feet away. He checked on her condition, then asked if she knew where Linda and Nancy were. Pam pointed in the direction of where the Andersons were carrying Linda to the car. Pam told her brother that one of the men had told her to come with them, too, and that she should grab a hold of the leg of his pants so she didn't get lost. But Pam was too frightened to move and stayed near the front steps. She started to cry as she watched them carry her bloodied sister away.

Once the Andersons got to their vehicle, Ken turned around and saw Chuck picking Pam up in a cradle position and carrying her toward his vehicle. As he was putting Pam in the front seat, an unfamiliar voice in the distance called out Chuck's name, urging him to send for an ambulance when he got to the hospital.

Inside her brother's car, Pam sat in the front passenger's seat. Chuck repeatedly told her to lie down as he drove east out of the disaster scene. But Pam kept refusing, afraid she would get blood on the seat from the open wound on the front of her head. Chuck assured her it was okay and gently placed his hand on the back of her head and eased her into a lying position. Unsure of the extent of Pam's injuries, Chuck stopped at his mother's house since he was heading in that direction anyway. Betty was outside and preparing to go over to check on the girls when Chuck pulled up. Betty opened the passenger door and saw Pam lying in the seat. She could see her daughter wasn't in grave danger, but still needed medical attention. So she got in the car and told Chuck to drive to the hospital. Oliver and Marie Harbo,

Betty's parents, lived nearby and agreed to take care of Georgia, Abbie, and their cousin.

Once inside the car, Betty immediately inquired about Linda and Nancy. Chuck informed her that Linda was being taken to the hospital by two men in a car, but he had no idea how badly injured she was. Pam said she saw her older sister being carried and that she was bleeding "pretty bad."

The Andersons laid Linda down in the back seat of their car, placing her on the blanket that Harriet had initially wrapped around her. Linda was then informed that Pam had been located by her brother and that she was not critically injured. Despite now writhing in pain, Linda insisted she be let out of the car to look for Nancy. Ken insisted the little girl would be found since there were now a lot of volunteers and rescue workers in the area.

Linda's painful moans caused Ken to become nervous and drive faster. He knew the young lady in the back seat of his car might bleed to death and her life was in his hands. The hospital was less than a mile away, yet the drived seemed like an eternity to him.

This mileage marker north of Tracy is the place where the American Legion baseball team watched the tornado out of the windows of a school bus. It also is the spot that the author got the inspiration for *Out of the Blue*. (Photo by *Tracy Headlight Herald*)

Linda, left, and Nancy pose for a picture one month before the tornado. (Submitted photo)

An empty twenty-five-ton boxcar was blown two blocks by the tornado and came to rest at an intersection in a residential area of town. (Photo by *Tracy Headlight Herald*)

After wreaking havoc with Tracy moments earlier, the F5 tornado destroys a farm site two miles northeast of town before finally dissipating. (Photo by Eric Lantz)

A damaged boat and an overturned automobile were left sitting atop the ruins of the Tracy tornado. (Photo by *Tracy Headlight Herald*)

Before the three-story Tracy Elementary School was leveled by the tornado, it housed students for seven decades. (Photo courtesy of Wheels Across the Prairie Museum)

An aerial view shows workers hauling debris from the Tracy Elementary School site. (Photo by *Tracy Headlight Herald*)

A clock that once hung on the wall in a classroom at the Tracy Elementary School sits atop the rubble with the time stopped at 7:04 p.m. (Photo by *Tracy Headlight Herald*)

Stunned citizens view the demolished Tracy Elementary School a day after the tornado struck. (Photo by *Tracy Headlight Herald*)

Nancy Vlahos now rests at the Worthington Memory Garden Cemetery.
(Submitted photo)

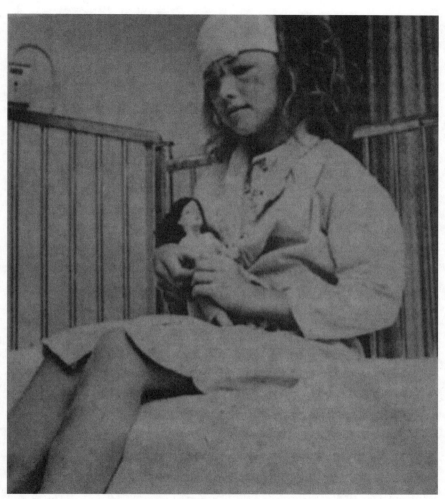

Pam Haugen, 8, sits on the edge of her hospital bed while being interviewed by a newspaper reporter. Pam was blown 350 feet from her home and then back again, yet suffered only minor injuries. (Photo by *Minneapolis StarTribune*)

Pam Haugen, left, and Linda (Haugen) Tordsen stand at the site of the Tracy Tornado Memorial forty-three years after the horrific night. (Photo by Scott Thoma)

Chapter 8

A TOWN DESTROYED

THE TORNADO EMBARKED ON TRACY and tore through it with the ease of a freshly sharpened chainsaw against a sapling. Nothing could stand up to the F5 fury. Homes, businesses, boats and cars were flung through the air in all directions. It slowed for a moment as it bulldozed its way through the three-story elementary school, then proceeded to make a large slice through the middle of town.

Bernie could feel the monster getting closer by the vibration in his basement on the north edge of town. The roaring of this vicious vortex was getting louder, indicating it was closing in on Bernie's neighborhood. Although the tornado's main power source was a block west of his house, Bernie felt as if his stomach was lifting from the pressure. For a brief moment, fear surfaced that he and his family would be taken from their home. But just as quickly, the feeling was gone and the noise from the storm was becoming less audible. Although their home suffered only moderate damage, the Holms' greenhouse 300 feet away was destroyed. Mayor Johnson's Gulf gas station just west of the greenhouse was also a total loss.

The tornado soon left Tracy, but not before hitting two more farms northeast of town and killing a man who had tried to outrun it in his car.

The wide-eyed occupants of bus number 22, still in their baseball uniforms, were now watching the elephant-trunk tornado cross the Airport Road in a northeasterly direction two miles in front of them. It appeared as though it was finally beginning to show signs of weakening as it became more elongated and thinner. But the tornado had second thoughts about retiring. It regrouped and continued for two more miles before finally dissipating for good.

Eric Lantz, a sixteen-year-old from Walnut Grove, captured some stunning photos of the tornado as it was leaving town. His uncle, Everett Lantz, owned the *Walnut Grove Tribune* at the time, and Eric often shot photos for the newspaper. With school out, he had even more time to venture out with his camera.

Eric was eating supper with his parents, Charles and Doris, when Everett came driving up to the house. Everette, in an excited voice, told his brother and nephew that he had just seen a huge white tornado in the vicinity of Tracy, seven miles to the west of Walnut Grove. Eric grabbed his Mamyia/Sykora 1000 TL camera he had purchased for $140 with his own money, and jumped in the front seat of his father's car. Charles quickly headed toward Tracy on County Road 7.

When Eric first saw the tornado leaving the Tracy city limits, he leaned out the window and shot a few pictures. Charles then stopped the car a quarter of a mile from town and Eric shot some photos standing outside on the side of the road. With blue sky behind him, he was able to take some quality shots before the tornado broke apart. The Lantzes then decided to continue into the city to take additional photos.

About the same time, Fritz Lessman was so nervous that he had trouble shifting the bus into gear to proceed into town. Because their minds were elsewhere, none of those aboard the bus even noticed Fritz's grinding of the gears. As Fritz finally began motoring the bus closer to town, branches and lumber were strewn across the road and everyone aboard become increasingly concerned of what might lie ahead. On a farm two miles outside of town, a horse in obvious agony was standing inside a fence with a large splintered board lodged halfway through its hind quarters, sending a chill down the spine of the passengers.

The players were now beginning to understand what had just happened to their city. Like a batter unable to dodge an inside fastball, Tracy had just been struck hard. Just outside of town, the players could now see the path the storm had taken as if a giant lawnmower had just been driven through town. Coach Bolin tried to comfort them as best he could. But he knew, too, that there were likely many people in town injured and possibly killed.

With the roads on the east side of town passable, except for the many branches and boards strewn across the roads, Fritz was able to make it into town with the bus. He stopped when he reached the intersection of the Airport Road and Highway 14, just two blocks east of the devastation. Six of the players aboard the bus who lived in the path on the west side of town had no knowledge of the well-being of any family members or if their homes were still intact. Not able to drive anyone in the direction where the storm came through town, the coach had no choice but to allow those six boys to get off the bus and walk home. Some had to walk over a mile through rubble to find their home. The coach had a sick feeling in the pit of his stomach, not knowing whether the players, who were like sons to him, would make it safely or if any of their families had been injured or killed. He also worried that they could be injured en route to their homes. But he didn't have a choice. The boys were frightened and wanted some answers. The coach wouldn't find out until several days later that one of his players had lost his home and his father and brother had been taken to the hospital with non life-threatening injuries.

Fritz continued driving the bus to the high school east of the storm's path and the remaining eight players got off to go home. Coach Bolin, recalling the bus passing by the wreckage of a friend's car and knowing his family sometimes visited a certain friend whose home was in the storm's path, jumped in his car and sped off for home on the east side of town. He would later find out that his wife and three children had gone into the basement of their home and were safe. Fritz walked to his home on the far west side of town through the rubble. Once there, he found his home and family were unscathed.

Bernie couldn't spend much time worrying about his business as he knew he was needed elsewhere. He was given a ride to the fire house by Police Chief Merle Kathman. There, he received information on which areas would need help and sent his men out to various locations to aid injured people, deal with the deceased and to also search through rubble for anyone missing. The town had four fire trucks. Bernie rode in the first engine to ravage-torn Greenwood, which he was told was in the hardest hit area. Of the sixty-two homes in this part of town, only twelve remained intact.

A second fire truck was sent to another section of Greenwood. One was sent to the elementary school area and another near where the railroad cars were toppled. Bernie also asked that several city workers go to the damaged areas with trucks and front-loaders and to also bring chainsaws and ropes.

Shortly after arriving in the Greenwood area, the truck Bernie was riding in stopped at a partially cleared intersection two blocks north of where Linda's house was. As Bernie jumped down from the truck, he was immediately met by a terrified woman who alerted him that a small child was lying dead in the street. She pointed to where the child lay a block away. Bernie grabbed a dark-brown blanket from the fire truck and headed toward the child, maneuvering through the branches and lumber in his route. Bernie approached the bloodied body of a small girl lying face-down. Even though he was sure the child was dead, he checked for vital signs. His initial thought was correct—there were no signs of life. He hung his head momentarily in sorrow. He hoped his intuition was wrong, but the veteran fire chief sensed there would be more scenes like this one.

Bernie looked at the child once more, but was unable to ascertain her identity. Her matching shirt and shorts were torn and stained with blood and dirt. The fatal blow most likely was the impact of her head hitting the pavement. Using the blanket as a makeshift body bag, Bernie carried the lifeless body toward the fire truck. Knowing he needed to keep looking for more people, Bernie flagged down John Dilly, who was driving a city truck in Greenwood. He gently placed the child's lifeless body in the back of the truck closest to the cab and asked John to take her to the hospital. Even though Bernie knew hauling her away in a city truck wasn't as respectful as he would have liked, but he felt the need to remove the body from the street was a consideration to the family so others wouldn't come upon it. Several people had spotted the toddler's body in the street and initially thought it was a doll.

Bernie and other workers administered first-aid to several injured residents of Greenwood before taking them to the hospital. None of the fire trucks carried stretchers aboard so rescue workers used doors or large boards they found lying atop the wreckage. Four men would then carry bodies on the makeshift stretchers and place them in the back of trucks or any available emergency vehicles.

All told, five deceased individuals were recovered in Greenwood and also were taken to the hospital. Many of the homes in this area were older and had no basements. All five of those killed in Greenwood were not in a basement at the time the tornado hit. Two of the bodies were recovered 100-or-more yards away from their home in a field. Two others were found amongst the rubble near their homes.

Soon, citizens throughout the town were assisting in the search and recovery of those trapped under debris. Many of the volunteer workers received injuries from nails protruding through broken boards, glass, and splintered wood. But most just continued working throughout the night before administering to their own needs.

Bernie was well-organized and orchestrated his men as if he had been through ordeals like this many times before. His deployment of members of the fire department throughout the city likely saved more lives. Bernie was often faced with having to make quick decisions on the spot and almost always made the right call. Surprisingly, no fires started anywhere in town, most likely because the downed power lines were dead with the city's 69,000-volt power line having been knocked out by the tornado south of town.

After everyone in the Greenwood area was accounted for, Bernie and his crews moved to Highway

14 to help clear a path for rescue vehicles arriving from neighboring cities into damaged areas of town. Men were placed at each intersection to keep traffic moving.

Local volunteers joined firemen and policemen in house-to-house checks to find out if anyone was missing or needed medical attention. Three complete cycles of inspections were made by emergency workers, who worked late into the night.

Police, state patrolmen, National Guardsmen and civil defense workers from various towns near Tracy were arriving to lend a hand and give exhausted workers a much-needed break.

While the city fire and police crews were working feverishly to assist or search for those injured or killed by the storm, a group of emergency personnel from Marshall, twenty-one miles away, were the first outsiders on the scene to augment local authorities. They played a vital role in maintaining order in Tracy. Marshall Police Chief Chet Wiener and Fire Marshal Mel Hardy followed shortly after, having been informed by state troopers who saw the tornado about to hit Tracy. While en route to Tracy, Hardy radioed to other firehouses in neighboring cities, asking for help and to provide Tracy with generators, lights, blankets, and drinking water. Firemen from Marshall and Pipestone were manning pumpers and standing by in case a fire broke out. Other firemen came in trucks or in their own vehicles from all over the region, including Balaton, Cottonwood, Currie, Fulda,

Garvin, Granite Falls, Lamberton, Minneota, Montevideo, Slayton, Walnut Grove, Westbrook, and Win-
dom.

Lyon County civil defense director I.J. Baumann, who lived in Tracy, was also providing invaluable assistance, informing the incoming volunteers
where they were needed and what their duties would
be. Most of the crews worked through the night, taking turns getting a few hours of rest. Most of the
workers were able to forge ahead with the physical
requirements. Mentally, though, they were drained
after witnessing the pain and agony the people of
town were going through. Bernie was among this
group.

The town was in ruins. The sudden impact had
everyone in despair. Never before had they witnessed
such an event. Just minutes before, everything was
standing. Now, a three-block area had been flattened.
Electrical lines were everywhere on the ground like a
bowl of pasta had been accidentally spilled on the
floor. And electrical and telephone lines were man-
gled and twisted in trees like cobwebs. People were
afraid they would be electrocuted or that sparks
would set off the natural gas lines now exposed in the
stricken areas. But Northern States Power employees
sent word that the wires were not "hot" because the
town's main power line had been taken out by the
twister.

People were aware that their homes and businesses could be repaired or rebuilt. And they were

well aware that their automobiles could be restored or replaced. But nothing could bring back the deceased. And nine of their friends, family or neighbors' lives were lost and the unwelcome monster showing no remorse for its actions.

As residents began emerging from the sanctity of their basements in the aftermath of the storm, initial concern was for those injured or unaccounted for.

Women could be heard screaming throughout the damaged areas. Some were screaming out of fear or shock, while others were screaming for someone to help with those injured. The screaming, followed by dogs barking almost in unison, frightened children who struggled to grasp the event that had just occurred in their town.

A fine gray powder hung in the air for several hours after the storm and was accentuated by the sunlight that followed the tornado. Many attributed it to the elementary school that had just been demolished. It also was likely from other building and other items the tornado accumulated during its journey. Many people in the path of the storm, as well as those assisting in that area, were covered with dirt and silt from head to toe, similar to the images of those people in or near the Twin Towers after the September 11, 2001, terrorist attacks.

The demolished elementary school in the center of the destruction was drawing the most attention. The storm's strength sheared off the top story of the three-story building. The second floor was left with gaping holes in the walls, while the first floor was filled with bricks, lumber, and school supplies from the top two floors. People from all over town were standing in disbelief amongst the rubble in front of the school whose front doors faced north to Harvey Street. Many of these people had once attended the school or had children that had just attended two weeks earlier. The concrete playground was filled with piles of tree branches, bricks, desks, and other school paraphernalia. Swing sets, slides, and monkey bars were bent to the ground or forcibly removed, leaving gaping holes where they were once anchored. The many elm trees along the south, west and north sides of the school had either been uprooted, blown apart or completely stripped of their leaves. Through one of the gaping walls on the west side of the school, a large school clock still clung to the wall of a class-room. The clock had stopped at 7:04 p.m. That clock, as well as others found in piles of wreckage, became indicators to the time the town was struck. The clock was shown on several television station newscasts in Minnesota and surrounding states. Photos of the clock also accompanied stories that appeared in countless newspapers and magazines throughout the country as a symbol of the time the town was pummeled.

Vernon Grinde, the elementary principal, made his way to the school on foot from his home four blocks away two hours after the tornado left town. He ran into Ralph Bierman, the school's janitor, and asked him to accompany him to examine the damage. The two men stared in disbelief at the fallen school. Tears welled up in Vernon's eyes as he noticed the clock clinging to the wall. He likened a smashed world globe that he saw atop the rubble outside the school to the way the town looked . . . as if the world had just ended.

Vernon was unable to sleep that night and ventured back outside at 5:00 a.m., this time to return to school to check on the students' files and other records kept in the office. Once there, Vernon worked his way inside the school with the help of National Guardsmen who were patrolling that area. Vernon lost his footing more than once while stepping over piles of bricks and other debris, but eventually made his way into the main office. A sense of relief came over the principal when he discovered the school's records were still safely tucked away inside the dented and scratched file cabinets. It was then that he realized what could have happened if the tornado had struck during the day two weeks earlier while school was still in session.

The school property's largest elm tree that stood on the southwest corner of the lot, bravely remained standing despite having its huge branches broken downward. The bare tree that once stood tall and full of leaves for many generations of pupils, now looked like a peeled banana with the biggest branches all bent down over the trunk.

Typically on a summer's evening, a janitor, teacher, or administrator might have been in the school catching up on paperwork, cleaning, or taking care of other administrative things. But, since the school had no air conditioning, the heat and humidity of the day likely swayed anyone's decision to go to the school and possibly saved lives.

Pam had just completed second grade. Her classroom was on the heavily damaged second floor. Had school still been in session, it was likely Pam and/or many others would have been seriously injured or even killed. In tornado drills throughout the years, children were advised to huddle in the hallways against a solid wall or to seek refuge under a heavy desk. But the school's top floor had been sheared off and the second floor was gutted, leaving the hallways and classrooms filled with bricks, beams, girders, and other paraphernalia.

Tracy did not have ambulance service in 1968. Instead it relied on two funeral homes in town to provide ambulance service with their station wagons.

John Almlie, who owned a furniture store for many years in Tracy, was also one of the town's funeral directors. He was home when he heard the siren blaring in town, but would soon be informed that his services were needed. John and his family lived on the east side of town, which was unharmed, but the Kelley-Almlie Funeral Home was near the damaged area. John drove his car over to the funeral home, and although the business was not heavily damaged, he was unable to access the station wagon that served the city as both an ambulance and a hearse. Debris had piled up in front of the garage door. So he drove to the furniture store he also owned in the business district, a block east of the storm's path. There, he hopped in the flatbed truck used for making furniture deliveries to his customers. He drove two blocks west to a severely damaged area and began loading injured citizens in need of medical attention on the back of the truck. Uninjured volunteers hopped in the back of the truck, too, to support the injured riders and make their journey as comfortable as possible and as a preventative measure so no one would fall off the truck. With ten injured people and six volunteers on the back of the truck, John made his way east to the hospital. He was able to maneuver the International truck through or over the rubble-filled roads, but the moaning coming from those injured meant the trip was anything but smooth. Never would John have thought that the truck he used for delivering beds, couches, or chairs would also be used to deliver injured citizens to the hospital.

Once arriving at the hospital, the injured were unloaded at the emergency entrance, and soon John headed back to the storm-ravaged section of town to pick up more injured and/or deceased citizens.

Vernon Butson of the Oman-Butson Funeral Home was able to get his station wagon out of the garage and also picked up people injured or dead. Fritz, who made sure his family was safe after dropping off the baseball team at the high school, rode with Vernon to assist him. Fritz, who owned a canvas repair shop in town, also was a gravedigger and was associated with both funeral directors in town.

National Guardsmen and ambulances eventually made their way to town from communities such as Marshall, Redwood Falls, and Pipestone to assist exhausted workers in Tracy. A rescue truck with a generator unit was dispatched immediately from Granite Falls. Many doctors, nurses and even veterinarians from nearby towns volunteered their services.

Fearing that out-of-towners would come in and begin looting, Tracy policemen, along with the help of police personnel from Marshall and several members of the Minnesota State patrol, set up roadblocks on all roads leading into Tracy. Only residents, relatives, and emergency workers were allowed in. Very little looting occurred with so many volunteer patrolmen standing guard. One man was caught attempting to steal meat from a deep freeze still sitting in the basement of a damaged home. Money could be found lying around everywhere in town. Citizens were urged to turn in any money they found to relief booths set up for those that lost homes and personal items.

The town was left with no electricity, water, or phone service for several hours. The water tower was spared by the puissant twister, but city officials decided that the town's water supply should be turned off until all the missing individuals were accounted for. They feared that if some were still trapped under the wreckage, they could drown if a busted water pipe filled their basement. Water was later transported into town from Slayton and Marshall in trucks until the city decided to turn the town's supply back on.

Northwestern Bell was on the scene within a few hours to set up temporary phone booths in front of their building to allow citizens to call out-of-town friends and relatives of the situation. The phone company's building was on the edge of the path of the storm and suffered roof damage and several broken windows.

The American Red Cross, along with many volunteers, fed those people left homeless, as well as providing nourishment to the many volunteers and city workers. The Red Cross workers were among the first groups of volunteers on the scene. Within hours, they set up disaster relief headquarters in the Tracy Municipal building. More than 350 families were affected in some way by the tornado and the Red Cross was ready to assist them. The Red Cross workers were also a welcome relief for Tracy Hospital employees, who were tirelessly attempting to treat the many injured patients. Aside from providing medical assistance to those with minor injuries — cuts and scrapes — the Red Cross medical team was also giving out tetanus shots. And, along with services provided by the Seventh Day Adventist Society, the Red Cross donated more than 500 articles of clothing and over 100 blankets to those left homeless. Some of the homeless slept that night on the floor inside the Armory, while others stayed at friends' or relatives' houses unaffected by the tornado.

Food lines lit up by lanterns were also set up in the Tracy High School's cafeteria by the Red Cross

SCOTT THOMA

and Salvation Army, providing hot meals to victims and workers. Often, the meal consisted of sandwiches, hot dogs, barbecues, beans, potato salad, soup, chips, cookies, bars, fruit, milk, and coffee. In all, an average of 815 people per day assisted more than 1,100 people with other various needs. The 7-Up Bottling Company donated pop for those volunteering with cleanup.

The Presbyterian Church also served food donated from members of their congregation and from other church groups. And volunteers from surrounding communities set up food stands outside in various locations, serving hot and cold food.

With the dust settled, the damage in Tracy could be assessed. There were 115 homes damaged, including seventy-six that had major damage. Five businesses were destroyed and another fifteen were structurally damaged. There were also ninety barns, garages and sheds damaged. And nearly 125 vehicles, three tractors, and a combine were damaged or totaled. According to insurance adjusters' tallies, the damage estimate for the city was over four million dollars, a number that would likely be ten times that amount in today's economy.

Minnesota Governor Harold LeVander arrived in Tracy on Friday, the day after the storm. Included in his entourage was administrative assistant Dave Durenberger, who would later become a United States state senator. Also, U.S. Senators Eugene McCarthy and Edmund Muskie came to Tracy

103

on Saturday to assess the damage. LeVander declared Tracy a state disaster area, meaning the town would receive funds to help with cleanup and restoration.

With the help of 160 local National Guardsmen, as well as city workers and countless volunteers, Tracy pulled up its virtual bootstraps and began rallying to clean up the destruction as quickly as possible. The townspeople refused to wave a white flag and tried its best to erase the footsteps of this beast of nature that invaded its territory. Tracy Mayor Dale Johnson, city council president Jack Von Bokern and other city council members agreed that the sooner the rubble was removed, the sooner citizens could try to return to some sort of semblance.

The buzzing of chainsaws and the roar of front-loaders dumping loads into trucks became a common reverberation for weeks after the tornado had hit. Airplanes and helicopters flew overhead daily for weeks, surveying the damage or taking photographs for newspapers and magazines. Instead of each resident being assigned to clean up his or her own property as was the norm after a storm, the mayor and city council members decided to have the city do the legwork. Workers in bulldozers, front-loaders, cranes, and backhoes worked feverishly to erase the horrific memory. There was a steady stream of traffic to and from the brush dump.

As odd as it seemed, the cleanup was happening too quickly for some. Some residents took longer than others to get over the shock or were dealing with an injured family member or the death of a loved one, feared that when they returned to their homes to sift through the rubble on their property for photos or other sentimental belongings, city crews might have already removed some or all of their wreckage.

But the mayor and city officials, many of them having their own homes or businesses damaged, made sure they were pushing all the right buttons in an attempt to keep the town's citizens as upbeat as possible. The officials reacted as quickly as possible to anyone's request or objection, no matter how big or small. Sometimes, however, it became a bit overwhelming with floods of requests. But the town had banded together like never before. Neighbors at odds before the event forgot about things as insignificant as a fence built too close to their property and were suddenly helping each other clean up the rubble. Residents living in Greenwood who had always felt like they were just people "on the other side of the tracks" were touched by the outpouring of support. Swarm of volunteers spread out through the town to help with recovery or clean-up.

This tornado ripped apart buildings as if they were made of balsa wood. It tossed steel girders around as if they were paper clips. And it crumbled the elementary school as if the bricks were molded from Styrofoam. Moments earlier, Tracy was a relatively obscure town in the Midwest. Now, it was the state's main attraction and was getting top billing on local, state and national news telecasts, radio stations and newspapers throughout the United States.

Bernie worked until 6:00 a.m. Friday, then decided to go home and attempt to get a little sleep and to inform his family of the horrific details that the town had thrust upon it. On his way home, he was amazed to see countless bulldozers, front-loaders, trucks and heavy equipment lined up on streets, all from neighboring towns. Many volunteer workers were inside their vehicles sleeping while waiting for sunrise to help the town clean up the mess. It would be a long and painful process. Although the tornado lasted only a few minutes, the town would take years to fully recover from the devastation.

The entire city showed an indefatigable spirit. But the fact remained that there were nine members of the community dead. No amount of cleanup or restoration would bring them back. The memory of this catastrophic night would forever be engrained in townspeople's minds.

Chapter 9

FILLED TO CAPACITY

N OT LONG AFTER PHONING THE DISPATCHER, Delpha was certain many people would be in need of medical attention in Tracy. Just from watching the powerful churning, it was easy for the farm family to ascertain this was going to be a night to remember.

Delpha had been a special duty nurse for critical patients at the Tracy Hospital for over twenty years. Normally, in emergency situations such as injuries sustained from a car accident or if a house fire had caused injuries to occupants or firemen, Delpha would be called in to assist doctors. This time, however, she knew she would be needed as quickly as possible. She asked Melvin to drive her to the hospital. Their sons, Allan and Bruce, wanted to ride along so they could see what had happened.

When the Kochs came upon the city, it looked to them like a war zone. The dust was still hovering a few feet above the ground as if a bomb had just been detonated. Nearly everyone they saw outside was covered in silt from head to toe. After seeing the damage, Delpha informed Melvin not to expect her back home for a long while. She was accustomed to tragedies in her line of work, but nothing compared to what she was now looking at with her mouth agape.

Upon arriving at the hospital, Delpha was met by several cars, trucks, and ambulances, all carrying injured townspeople. She helped some of them inside the hospital and then went to get cleaned up to begin her duties. But she was told by other nurses that the hospital was without water. Doctors and nurses had to scrub up with a disinfectant called Zephirin. Dri-wipes were also used before members of the medical staff put on rubber gloves.

The hospital's main phone line was in working order and receptionist Meribel Steiner put out calls for water to those she felt could help. Within thirty minutes, several farmers dropped off water tanks in the back of the hospital. Nurses had to go outside to retrieve the water like pioneer women with buckets down by a stream.

Dr. Norman Lee and Dr. Roger Schroeppel were the primary physicians at Tracy Hospital. Dr. Patrick Bosley of Balaton, a surgeon, was also on staff. And Dr. Charles Graham, a radiologist from Spirit Lake, Iowa, worked at the hospital in Tracy once a week.

Dr. Lee was at his home at the time the tornado struck. With his house several blocks from the path, he was able to take several photos from his front yard and even captured a few seconds of the twister with his eight-millimeter video camera as it churned through the city. Lee's video was eventually obtained by CBS Television and used on the air by renowned newscaster Walter Cronkite. With the twister gone and knowing the city had been hit hard, Dr. Lee headed for the hospital.

At the time the tornado struck town, there were five nurses on duty at the hospital working a scheduled 3:00 to 11:00 p.m. shift. Dr. Schroeppel had just completed his rounds and was about to go home for the evening.

Dr. Lee and Dr. Schroeppel reached the hospital doors within minutes of the tornado leaving town. Patients were starting to come in and the two physicians sensed there would be an overload of patients and that more assistance would be required. Retired doctor Warner G. Workman, who was eighty years old and had been a physician in Tracy for five decades, volunteered his services. Lee asked a nurse to have someone attempt to locate Dr. E.K. Bicek and Dr. Donald Hicks, the town's veterinarians, to see if they were available to come to the hospital and assist. Lee and Schroeppel concurred that the veterinarians' medical training would be invaluable to the situation. Dr. Bicek was available and immediately came in to help, but Dr. Hicks was a member of the fire department and was already on a truck helping those injured or searching for those unaccounted for. Dr. Bosley lived twelve miles from Tracy and headed for the hospital in his car as soon as he heard the news. Dr. Graham boarded a private plane and flew to Tracy that same night.

The Anderson vehicle, transporting Linda, was one of the first to arrive at the hospital. Ken Anderson drove into the emergency entrance where hospital personnel placed Linda onto a gurney and brought her into the emergency room where Delpha immediately began checking her vital signs. Nurses tried to coagulate the most severe bleeding in Linda's right ankle and foot, left leg, and her head. They noticed Linda's right ankle was twisted completely backwards and a large tear was present going in all directions. Nearly all of the skin and subcutaneous tissue, or the layer just below the skin, were gone around the ankle. Dr. Bosley prepped for surgery as soon as he learned the extent of Linda's injuries.

Linda was writhing in pain, and it was assumed that she was going into shock. Dr. Bicek, accustomed to stitching animals at his veterinarian's office, sutured Linda's most serious gashes to quell her bleeding before she could get into surgery. He also administered a shot of Demerel to relieve her discomfort as nurses tried to clean the embedded dirt and blood off her as best they could in an attempt to stave off infection.

Using shortwave radios, policemen from Tracy and other towns already on the scene, made calls to neighboring cities asking for additional medical personnel. Four doctors from Marshall, four from

Slayton, and two from Pipestone, as well as a dentist from Walnut Grove, arrived within hours to lend a helping hand. Countless nurses from several surrounding communities arrived within hours to volunteer their services. Without any hesitation upon hearing the tragedy on television, three nurses from Duluth united and drove the five-hour trip to Tracy and were on hand shortly after 1:00 a.m. Many of the out-of-town doctors brought medical supplies with them as requested by emergency personnel.

As soon as the tornado was safely out of town, there was constant movement all over town.

Nellie Wright, the director of Nursing, went directly to the hospital the moment the tornado left town.

Linda's sister, Kathy, heard about the tornado on television and immediately drove to Tracy from her home in Jeffers, thirty-five miles from Tracy.

Linda's father, after finding out that Linda and Pam were injured, quickly headed to the hospital from his repair shop.

Susan arrived at Campbell's Soup Company in Worthington just before 8:00 p.m. for her shift that night, having no knowledge of what had just happened in Tracy. Co-workers who knew Linda was adopting her daughter, were shocked to see Susan at work. When they informed her of the tornado, Susan didn't even bother to tell anyone she was leaving. She scurried out the door to get into her car to make the hour-long drive to find out if Linda and Nancy were safe.

When Susan arrived in Tracy, she headed straight for the Greenwood section. Once there, she could see the entire area had been pounded hard. The view left her nervous and scared. She tried to drive into the area where Linda's house was, but patrolmen would not allow her entrance. She pleaded with the patrolmen and explained that her friend and daughter lived there. The patrolmen checked his list of those accounted for and informed Susan that they had been taken to the hospital, but had no other information available.

The Tracy Municipal Hospital employed thirty-five nurses. By midnight all but two of the hospital employees, scheduled or not, were at the scene within the hour. That included nurses, janitors, cooks, maintenance workers, and receptionists. The two unable to make it to work that night because they were out of town on family vacation, returned the next day.

It had been an unusual day at the hospital. Normally, the forty-two-bed facility built in 1962 would have an average of fifteen occupants that required an overnight stay. On June 13, however, there were already thirty-five beds occupied with patients before the tornado had even entered town. That left only seven beds vacant for the many injured from the tornado before and after being treated. The hospital staff saw 100 injured patients the night of June 13. Of those, twenty-three required an overnight stay, while the others were treated and released. All elective surgery at Tracy Hospital had to be postponed for an additional week to allow for those in need of immediate surgical procedures from the storm or in the aftermath. The staff treated patients with fractured vertebra, fractured limbs, chest injuries, lacerations and abrasions, concussions, and puncture wounds. Surgical tools were "cold sterilized" with no way to heat the water. In all, 171 tornado-related patients went through the outpatient department. Nearly one fourth of those had puncture wounds from stepping on or being hit by nails protruding from boards.

Two National Guardsmen were posted at the hospital, one at the main entrance the other to direct traffic and to also keep the ambulance entrance clear. But many of the drivers of vehicles were in such a hurry to get their injured passengers inside the hospital that they turned a deaf ear to the guard and parked anywhere they found a space available.

With power out throughout the town, the hospital relied on small standby generators for lights in the emergency room, operating room, and patient areas. Flashlights were seen shining throughout the hospital.

By now, wounded patients were coming through the hospitals doors like shoppers at a department store the day after Thanksgiving. Some walked in with assistance, others were carried in on doors or pieces of large wood. Sometimes it became a struggle getting the makeshift stretchers through the doors. Many of the vehicles that transported the injured to the hospital arrived with flat tires, punctured by glass, nails, and other sharp objects on the debris-filled roads along the route. One vehicle arrived with all four tires flattened, yet the driver managed to "rim" it to the hospital.

Wright, a former Army nurse, had set up the hospital dining room as a triage where the medical staff could determine the priority of patients' treatment based on the severity of their condition. The dining room was used to place most of the incoming patients because natural light was still available through a large window. Flashlights and lanterns were then used when it became dark outside. A large generator brought in from Granite Falls was available by morning, and power was restored throughout the hospital.

Linda was one of only two patients to undergo surgery the same night the tornado hit. Dr. Bosley performed four hours of surgery on her that night. Surgical nurse Dolly DeBlieck, who had already witnessed two of her neighbors dead before she headed to the hospital, assisted Dr. Bosley.

With her mother holding a towel to her head to stop the bleeding, Pam was driven to the emergency entrance by her brother. She was also one of the early arrivals. Pam was taken to the dining room, but because of her age and because she had sustained a head injury, she was among the first patients to receive treatment by a doctor.

With the sudden overload of patients, extra beds and bedding from the Christian Manor Nursing Home and the Tracy Nursing Home were brought into the hospital. Even some camping cots were delivered by neighboring residents in case they were needed. Five critically injured patients were treated first. Each would get one of the available hospital rooms to make it easier for doctors to have access to them following treatment. Others with less severe injuries were placed on beds or cots in hallways after all the hospital's rooms had been filled. It was not a day for modesty. Patients undressed in front of one another in the hallways to allow doctors to move from one patient to another as quickly as possible. Many of the severely injured patients had been stripped of parts of their clothing by the force of the wind and, without that protection, when they were brought into the hospital, they looked like they had been wrestling with a bobcat.

Nearly all of the injured people brought in were blackened by silt and dirt, which, along with blood, was ground into the sheets and pillow cases on their cots or beds. The patients' eyes were swollen and red from tiny particles having made their way into them.

John Dilly, whom Bernie had asked to bring the little girl's lifeless body to the hospital, arrived at the emergency entrance, and hospital volunteers took the blanketed child from the back of the truck and carried her inside where they were told to bring her to the laundry room. Due to limited space in other rooms and a need for privacy, hospital personnel covered the bodies of those killed with blankets or sheets and placed them on tables in the laundry room. They would remain there pending a positive identification. Eight of the nine killed were brought into the hospital that night. The ninth victim was found the next day and brought in.

With adrenal glands working in high gear and because patients were screaming and moaning, hospital workers admitted they never felt fatigued until the number of injured patients being brought in began to decline early the next morning. By then, nurses from other communities were providing relief. Still, the Tracy Hospital staff members would only sleep for a few hours and then return for additional duty. They felt a sense of obligation to treat patients, many who were their friends.

Chapter 10
"THAT'S NOT MY SISTER."

IT WAS SURPRISING THAT PAM only sustained a slight concussion from hitting her head on the doorway while being blown out of the house. Her head, just behind the hairline, received a three-inch gash that Dr. J.E. Eckdale, a Marshall doctor who volunteered his services, sutured. She also had a large laceration that ran from her forehead to the bridge of her nose in a triangular pattern. Pam was diagnosed with a mild concussion, but X-rays were negative for a skull fracture.

Two small cigarette drains were inserted in the scalp lacerations. Nurses wrapped a gauze bandage around Pam's head, cleaned up her scrapes and gave her a tetanus shot. She was also treated for multiple soft tissue injuries. Considering what she had been through, it was even more surprising that none of Pam's injuries were considered severe.

Linda wasn't as fortunate. But because she was taken to the hospital so quickly, Dr. Lee reported, she was able to overcome her injuries.

Clifford's parents, Virgil and Dolores Vaske, lived in Adrian at the time of the tornado and were in Tracy by 9:00 p.m. after hearing the news of the torthe radio. They brought along their daughter, Debbie, who had been staying at Linda's house for a few days in Tracy and was planning to stay through the weekend, but had had a change of heart and called her parents to come and get here the day before the tornado. Upon arriving in Tracy that night, they were also denied entrance into Greenwood and instead directed to go to the hospital.

John Schleppenbach, the pharmacist who had filled a prescription that Linda brought in earlier in the day, was trained as a medic in the National Guards and volunteered his services to the hospital. Dr. Lee asked John to identify as many of the deceased as he could, including a little girl killed in the Greenwood area. John had a feeling it might be Nancy. When the cloth was pulled down to reveal the face of the little girl lying on a table, he fought back tears. She looked asleep and at peace. He knew immediately it was the same girl that had been in his store just two hours earlier. He identified her as Nancy Vlahos.

As Betty was waiting in the hospital for any news about her daughters, she asked a woman at the reception desk if anyone had brought a little girl into the hospital. Betty explained that her daughter was caring for the child and planned to adopt her. The receptionist told her to wait a few moments while she checked with the proper personnel. A few minutes later, a member of the hospital staff came out and took Betty into a private area, informing her that a little girl had been killed by the tornado and that she had been identified as Nancy Vlahos.

Betty was devastated at the news. She loved the little girl and had been eagerly awaiting the day Clifford and Linda would have the adoption completed. Betty was even more worried about Linda now. She hadn't been told of the extent of Linda's injuries, but was informed that she was in surgery.

Linda and Pam's father, Clarence, arrived at the hospital shortly after they were brought in. Chuck and Betty filled him in on what they knew at that point.

Pam was given one of the vacant patient rooms since she was one of the early arrivals and also because doctors wanted to monitor her head injury. After an hour wait, her family members were told that they could go into Pam's room. Pam looked like she was wearing an oversized headband and the skin on her legs showing under her light blue robe were full of bruises and small red marks that looked like measles.

With tears still welled up in her eyes, Betty told Pam that Nancy didn't make it. Pam didn't know how to react as she had never faced death before. It was hard for her to imagine never getting to play with the little girl again. She then asked her how Linda was, but became frightened when she was told that her big sister was in surgery and had lost a lot of blood. Silently to herself, Pam prayed for Linda to be okay.

Virgil and Dolores eventually arrived at the hospital and also were admitted to Pam's room. They, too, were told the solemn news of Nancy's death. Red Cross workers on hand at the hospital then got in touch with Clifford's unit in Washington and told the commanding officer the news about the tornado and his wife. Clifford was eating his evening meal in the mess hall when he was told there was an emergency back home and that he should go to the command post for more information. Clifford ran to the command post and was told by the officer that there was a phone call for him. Clifford was shocked and initially didn't believe the caller's information.

Arrangements were made by the Red Cross for Clifford to be granted a one-week pass to get to Tracy. He was on an airplane early the next morning.

When Susan arrived at the hospital later that night, she went to the registration desk and informed Meribel who she was and why she was there. Meribel then called for a nurse or doctor to come out to speak to Susan. Two nurses brought Susan into a room and told her the sad news about her daughter. She sobbed as she plopped down into a chair.

When Linda got out of surgery that night, Susan requested that she be allowed to see her friend. But because she wasn't an immediate family member and because Linda was still in intensive care, Susan was not allowed. Susan felt alone and unsure what to do. She briefly chatted with Betty and , then decided to drive back to Worthington.

The surgery on Linda's ankle and toes went better than expected. It was initially feared she could lose either or both because of the severity of the injury.

Linda had a compound fracture/dislocation of her right ankle. Her talar bone (the flat bone on top of the heel bone) was fractured and she had extensive soft tissue damage. Bosley removed the dead, damaged and infected tissue to improve the healing of the remaining healthy tissue in the ankle and heel. He then relocated the ankle bones as well as possible. A small portion of her fourth toe was removed and the area sutured. The little toe, torn partly off, was sutured and saved.

Dr. Richard Hederstrom, who also came over from Marshall to lend a hand, then worked on Linda's left leg. Despite a four-inch cut completely through the calf muscle, there were no fractures. Hederstrom repaired the damaged muscle and sutured Linda's leg. It was hard to determine what went through her leg, but doctors figured it was something metal and flat.

Linda had two deep lacerations on her skull. The anterior, or front of her head, was lacerated two inches down to bone just behind her hairline. The posterior had a large Y-shaped laceration down to bone.

Doctor Bosley also was closely monitoring Linda for a possible ruptured spleen.

After several hours in recovery, Linda was placed in a private room. Her family was allowed to visit her, but few words were spoken. Clarence thought his daughter looked like she had been shot with a twelve-gauge shotgun because her entire body was full of bruises, cuts, scrapes, and pock marks.

Linda was nearly unrecognizable with her head swollen to nearly twice its normal size. When her sister Kathy arrived at the hospital later that night, she checked in at the front desk and asked a receptionist what room Linda Vaske was in. The receptionist checked her chart and told Kathy to go to Room 106.

When Kathy peeked in the door to Room 106, she didn't recognize the woman on the bed and thought to herself "That's not my sister." No one else was in the room as her mother and brother were visiting with Pam. So Kathy went back out into the hallway to ask someone else. There, Kathy spotted her father and was told that she had been given the right room number.

Kathy went back to Room 106 and, even after standing next to Linda's bed, still was unable to recognize the heavily-sedated body laying there as her sister.

Clifford arrived in Tracy the next day and immediately went to the hospital. Linda was still in intensive care and her nervous husband couldn't believe how his bride of only ten months looked like she had been in a war zone. He doubted there was more than an inch anywhere on her body without a cut, scrape, or bruise.

With Susan back home in Worthington, she contacted the Wallin Funeral Home early the next morning to begin arrangements for transporting Nancy's body back to Worthington for burial. Darle Wallin, the funeral director, contacted the Tracy Hospital to arrange for the body to be picked up and transported back to Worthington.

There was no funeral at a church for the little girl. Instead, the Wallin Funeral Home conducted a memorial service at 10:30 a.m. on June 17, four days after the tornado.

No members of Susan's immediate family attended the memorial service because of their estranged relationship following her pregnancy. Many of Susan's friends and acquaintances, though, were on hand to pay their respects. Clifford chose not to attend because he had only a few more days remaining on his military pass and he wanted to be near Linda as long as she was still in critical condition.

Linda and Pam's mother and their two youngest sisters, Georgia and Abbie, went to the ceremony, as did Clifford's parents and his sister. Pam, who had been released from the hospital the day before the funeral, stayed with her grandparents in Tracy.

Nancy was laid to rest in a white marble casket. The open casket revealed a little girl who looked like a porcelain doll. She was dressed in a frilly white dress with powder blue trimmings and powder blue socks.

The Reverend Theodore G. Predoehl presided over the brief ceremony at the funeral home, reminding those in attendance how short life can be and that each day should be lived to the fullest.

Nancy was buried in the Worthington Cemetery. A small understated blue and white marbled headstone marked her burial site. The inscription simply read:

Nancy Ann Vlahos
Jan. 8, 1966 – June 13, 1968.

The last time Linda saw Nancy was when she picked the little girl up from her crib before attempting to get to the basement. She never witnessed her lifeless body in the hospital. A friend took a picture of Nancy's closed casket at the cemetery and later gave it to Linda.

On Saturday, two days after the tornado swept through town, media representatives from all over the state, as well as some other states, were swarming through the town like ants around a colony. A reporter and photographer from the *Minneapolis Tribune*'s Sunday edition were granted permission to talk to Pam. As she sat on the edge of her bed, nervously twisting the hair of a doll she had received as a gift, Pam answered the interviewer's questions. Her picture accompanied a front-page story about the three girls blown from their house.

Linda remained in the hospital until July 17, then returned every five days for skin grafting until completion on August 12.

Clarence drove Linda to the site where her home once stood following her discharge in July. Being told repeatedly what to expect didn't suppress her element of surprise.

She could hardly believe her eyes. The Greenwood area had been entirely cleaned up. Little was left except open basements. Most of the homes and trees were gone. Green lawns were now just bare spots with visible large caterpillar treads everywhere.

Linda again looked at the lot where she had lived. With tears in her eyes, she couldn't believe everything was gone. And her thoughts turned to Nancy. She, too, was gone. Linda got back into her father's car and stared blankly out the window as he drove away.

Chapter 11
THE AFTERMATH

SEVERE WEATHER WAS RAMPANT in Minnesota and Iowa on June 13, 1968. The National Weather Service confirmed that there were thirty-seven funnel cloud or tornado sightings that day within a 300-mile radius of their bureau in Minneapolis.

A tornado caused moderate damage to ten homes and felled several trees in Montevideo that night. A greenhouse in Willmar had nearly 1,000 window panes broken by high winds. And a shopping center's roof collapsed in Spring Park due to high winds and torrential rain, pouring two inches of water throughout the inside of the store. There was also a confirmed report of a tornado touching down and causing damage to a dance hall and to an amusement park in Arnold's Park in Spencer, Iowa. Another tornado caused damage to at least five resort properties on West Okoboji Lake in Iowa.

Confirmed and unconfirmed reports of a tornado on the ground that day came from several witnesses near or in the Minnesota cities of Chaska, Clara City, Currie, DeGraff, Granite Falls, Janesville, Lamberton, LeCenter, LeSueur, Montevideo, Revere,

Sleepy Eye, Springfield, Storden, Wabasso, Waseca, and Westbrook. A second tornado touched down one mile north of Tracy ninety minutes after the F5 devastation occurred. A tornado was also verified between Fargo and West Fargo in North Dakota and Vermillion and Sioux Falls in South Dakota.

Despite all the other sightings of tornadoes, there was little talk of anything other than the one that plowed through Tracy.

Tornadoes are categorized into five magnitudes on the Fujita Scale or F-scale, named for Tetsuya Fujita, who co-introduced the damage scale in 1971 with partner Allen Pearson. The Fujita scale is a rating of the intensity of a tornado based primarily on the damage it inflicts on human-built structures and vegetation. Several other factors go into the determination of the scale assigned to a particular tornado such as eyewitness accounts, media reports, radar, ground-swirl pattern and photos and/or video of the actual tornado, if available. The official category magnitudes are determined by meteorologists following a ground and/or aerial survey. Meteorologists and engineers determined the category based on the damage. Experts rated tornadoes prior to 1971, including Tracy's, retroactively as far back as 1880. Each of the six (0-1-2-3-4-5) F-scale magnitudes determined the wind speed based on certain structure damage and weight of items lifted off the ground. An F4 tornado, for instance, generated winds between 207 and 260 miles per hour and could topple train cars. A tornado rated an F5 had wind speeds between 261 and 318 miles per hour and could lift automobiles and hurl them at least 109 yards or more, debark trees, and lift structures and disintegrate them in the air.

Meteorologists from St. Paul and Sioux Falls estimated the wind speeds generated by the tornado that hit Tracy to be well in excess of 300 miles per hour because of the way it lifted and tossed some railroad cars with ease and because of the way it leveled the structurally-sound elementary school. Tornadoes are now rated by an Enhanced Fujita Scale (EF) that began operational use in 2007.

Tracy's tornado hugged the ground its entire route, appearing to dissipate as it left town, but reformed for a few more seconds, then finally broke up for good at 7:12 p.m. According to the National Weather Service, this tornado churned along the ground at approximately thirty-five miles per hour for twenty-four minutes on the ground while covering a little over thirteen miles in parts of Lyon, Murray and Redwood counties. Meteorologist Joseph Strub estimated the tornado's damage zone to be around 500 feet. That included the damage core of 250 feet wide and lesser damage approximately 125 more feet on each side.

When Linda's father, Clarence, went to the Vaskes' rented home the day after the tornado hit to salvage any belongings left behind by the storm, he noticed the basement was full of items from a neighbor's home. According to an eyewitness, the neighbor's home was lifted from its foundation and literally exploded by the force of the wind. A water heater and a bathtub landed in the southwest corner of Linda and Clifford's basement. Had the girls made it into the southwest corner of the basement that evening, as Linda had planned, none of them may have survived. Clarence also noticed so much broken glass built up along the north side of the basement wall that it left the impression of a large snow drift.

Linda and Clifford lost nearly all of their belongings, including all their photos and other sentimental items that they would never be able to replace. The class ring that Linda placed on the window sill in the kitchen before she washed dishes prior to the storm was never found. All of Nancy's clothing and toys were blown away. One of the few items found was Linda's fur coat, which was badly stained and soiled. After several unsuccessful attempts to clean it, the coat was thrown away. A couple of days after the tornado, a utility worker found a pile of her jewelry on the ground nestled against a telephone pole. The jewelry box that once held the items was nowhere in sight.

Also found was one of Linda's puppies. The all-white mutt was found amongst the rubble at Arlo Ziemke's property, which was three lots west of the Vaskes' home. Arlo gave the puppy to Clarence, who kept it and appropriately named him Tornado.

Clifford's Thunderbird was found over 100 yards east of the road where it had been parked in front of the house. The once shiny red vehicle without a single scratch on it before the storm, was left looking as though a high-speed freight train rammed into it. The back end of the car was coiled up like an accordion.

But the Vaskes were not exclusive in having to cope with such extensive damage. Many families found themselves in the same situation with all their belongings having been snatched from them in an instance.

LeVander met with other state and local officials at the municipal building to discuss options for some type of disaster relief for the town. So overcome by the destruction scene, LeVander admitted to a television reporter that he cried after meeting with several citizens. He immediately utilized his authority and ordered state highway workers to bring in portable electric generators to assist the hospital and other areas that needed electricity the most. He declared the town a state disaster, allowing for state funds to help in the recovery process.

Minnesota Senator Eugene McCarthy, who was a presidential hopeful at the time, flew into Tracy with several Secret Service personnel, three days after the disaster. McCarthy filed a national disaster declaration with President Lyndon Johnson. But the declaration was denied because the town's damage estimate was not large enough to qualify.

Insurance adjusters estimated the damage between three and four million dollars—a figure likely to be ten times as large if the tornado occurred today, according to a USD inflation percentage. In all, 150 people were injured, 111 homes destroyed and an additional seventy-six homes suffered major damage. Five of the town's businesses were completely destroyed, while fifteen others suffered some type of damage. Unfortunately, many of the homeowners were not fully insured. Some had no insurance at all. But insurance companies were cooperative and assisted those as best they could with relocating or rebuilding. The state also provided assistance to business owners.

Levander, who had only been governor for one year when the tornado swept through Tracy, stopped at the hospital prior to leaving town. He briefly visited with doctors, nurses, and some of the injured patients, including Linda and Pam. Levander's visit was brief, but he wished them each a speedy recovery. He patted Pam on the shoulder, asked her how old she was, and told her not to be afraid.

The town slowly began to erase the appearance of a junk yard and a majority of the cleanup was completed in the first five days. Roadblocks were removed five days after the tornado, and sightseers from all over the country came in droves. It was as if shoppers were lined up outside a department store on Black Friday, all scurrying into town as soon as they were allowed to enter. According to one local airplane pilot who flew over the town to witness the wreckage, the vehicles of those curious sightseers were lined up as far back as two miles in either direction of Highway 14. The flow of traffic was so steady that it hindered city workers attempting to complete cleanup duties. Homeowners also found it a hindrance to run errands or to finish their own cleanup chores by bringing branches to the brush site because their vehicles were often blocked in. License plates from South and North Dakota, Iowa, Wisconsin, Nebraska, Illinois, Michigan, Montana, Nebraska, New York, Indiana, and Pennsylvania were noticed by those volunteering with traffic control.

But lifting the roadblocks wasn't all bad. Many of the people coming into town didn't arrive with empty arms. They brought food, clothing, blankets, toiletries, and cash donations. But most of all, they brought empathy and lifted the spirits of many of the downtrodden Tracy residents. The flux of volunteers into the community was almost hard to fathom. Helpful hands didn't just come from neighboring towns—they came from all over Minnesota and other states as well.

Over 1,000 teen-age volunteers from organizations such as Boy Scouts, Camp Fire Girls, 4H, and various church groups were placed in fields outside of town to help remove debris from existing crops. Over 1,000 aces of cropland had been ruined, according to a Lyon County Extension agent. The Red Cross would send canteen trucks to the fields to provide lunch to the volunteers.

One of the toughest tasks the town encountered was the removal of the twenty-six toppled train cars. A large wrecking company from Huron, South Dakota, was hired for the job. A large highway crane and two caterpillars were brought in from Mankato to assist. It took several days to complete the work order. Twelve of the cars were beyond repair and were hauled out on flatbed train cars and scrapped.

Also, it took hundreds of man hours to clear the wreckage from the elementary school. First, though, the school's principal, Vernon Grinde, his wife, Ruth, who was the school's librarian, and several other staffers and volunteers sifted through the wreckage in an attempt to salvage any items that could be used in future school years. Books able to be saved were minimal. Even those stored away for the summer had silt and glass between the pages despite being stacked on top of one another.

School personnel had just completed inventory on the school supplies before putting them away for the year. The inventory ledger was found in the files and proved invaluable in helping to settle losses with insurance adjusters. Neighboring school districts donated desks and other school supplies Tracy needed.

The removal of the rubble around the school went quickly. The remaining walls of the school were knocked down with a wrecking ball. When everything was hauled away, carpenters stepped in to construct seven temporary one-room buildings that were used as classrooms for the 1968-1969 school year. Grades four through six held classes in the identical-looking buildings, while the seventh building was used for a central meeting area and the cafeteria. The buildings, referred to as "huts" by the teachers, had two doors and two windows. And each had its own furnace, but had no air conditioning. Heated passageways linked the buildings.

Kindergarten and first-graders attended school in the Methodist Church and second-grade students held classes in the Tracy Lutheran Church. Pam and her fellow third-grade classmates, along with special education students, spent the following year at St. Mary's Catholic Church.

The "huts" were used for two full years and part of a third until the new grade school was completed south of town in January of 1971.

The bright white "huts" stood out and looked unusual beside each other north of where the former halcyon elementary school served for so many years.

As with many tornadoes, there were several unusual sightings in the aftermath of the one that pulverized Tracy.

Darold Johnson was one of the Greenwood residents who lost his home. After seeking refuge in the basement, Johnson sat down and leaned his back against a center support beam, placing his arms over his head in a protective position. In a matter of seconds, his home was gone as if a magician had performed a vanishing act. Johnson relaxed his arms and looked up. Instead of seeing the basement ceiling, he now saw blue sky. And when he turned around, the beam he was leaning against was also removed without his knowledge.

Paul Kretchmer's home was a block east of the tornado's path and sustained only minor damage. When Paul came out of the basement to inspect his house once the storm passed, he noticed a plastic soda straw was imbedded into the living room window. Half of the straw was inside the house and the other half was outside the house. The window was not cracked or shattered around the straw's penetration point. When the straw was removed, a perfect hole was seen in the glass with just minor chips around the edges.

Leaning up against Bob Silver's garage before the storm reached town were a pair of lightweight folding lawn chairs. The tornado took the entire garage, but left the lawn chairs on the ground next to the cement pad the building was stationed on.

In one large oak tree along east of the storm's path were three table knives and a fork stabbed into the center of the trunk in a diamond pattern. Knives and forks were also seen lodged into the sides of several undamaged homes a block away from the path

In one ravaged basement, a lonely open pantry was seen still hugging a south wall. Even though there was nothing else salvageable in the basement, the eighty-eight glass canning jars resting on the seven pantry shelves were untouched.

And plastic grass used for Easter baskets, was driven into the siding of one home with such force that it left marks when it was removed.

There were also cars and boats found in trees, a full carton of eggs found in the middle of a street with only one of the eggs cracked, a cat emerging from under the rubble in a basement two days after the storm and numerous other unusual sights throughout the damaged area.

Perhaps the most fitting item found in the aftermath was by Jerry Engesser. While cleaning up his yard, he noticed a hardcover book on top of the rubble. He leaned down and picked it up. Turning it over, he read the title on the front cover: *Gone with the Wind*.

Chapter 12
GONE, BUT NOT FORGOTTEN

DESPITE TRACY HAVING BEEN HAMMERED by one of the most powerful tornadoes in United States history, storm experts said the town was lucky more lives were not lost. But luck had nothing to do with it. It was the citizens' concern for one another that likely saved many more lives.

There were several factors that determined why a storm of this magnitude could hit the heart of a city and and not cause many more deaths or even many more severe injuries.

(1) While this particular tornado stayed on the ground much longer than most of those that are categorized as F5, the two- to three-block wide swath of the rotation was narrower than the average, thus sparing more homes and lessening the likelihood of more injuries or deaths.

(2) Because the tornado formed during daylight hours, many people saw it coming into town and were able to seek shelter or to warn others.

(3) The town was alerted in advance. Tornadoes can develop anywhere. They don't always form outside of town and then build up a head of steam before inflicting damage in town. They can just as easily

develop right on top of a town. The quick-thinking phone call from the Koch family was regarded as potentially saving hundreds of lives.

(4) There were others outside of town who saw the tornado and phoned friends and relatives in town, warning them of what was approaching.

(5) Strann Nelson, a policeman, drove up and down several streets in town with the car's siren blaring while also audibly warning people via the car's public address speaker system.

(6) The train workers who thought enough of the townspeople to risk their own lives by running the train back and forth on the track blowing the engine's whistle as a warning to heed the town's civil defense siren.

(7) Carson Johnson, a concerned citizen, drove his car through Greenwood and warned anyone he saw to seek shelter.

(8) Ubiquitous fire chief and civil defense director Bernie Holm and dispatcher Julius DeBlieck each remained calm in the line of duty and utilizing the warning system to perfection.

(9) The town's rescue units dispatched to ravaged areas immediately after the twister left the city limits to assist those in need of medical assistance.

(10) Neighbors, friends and relatives digging through splintered boards, sharp metal, and broken glass in search of those people unaccounted for.

(11) And the countless number of emergency workers and volunteers from other communities.

Each of the aforementioned unselfish acts likely minimized the number of fatalities. Some of the town's citizens who lost homes were firemen, rescue workers, and hospital personnel. After making sure family members were safe, they immediately tended to their civic duties in helping those in need and worrying about their own lost homes and treasures later.

Fortunate timing may have played a part, such as the tornado not developing two weeks earlier during school hours when elementary classrooms were filled with students and teachers.

Of the nine people who died in Tracy and/or its Greenwood suburban section, none were killed while in their basement or some other sort of storm shelter. Some, however, had been in the basement but decided for one reason or another to go back upstairs before the storm had passed. The stories of how and why they were killed have varied over the years. I still remember the trembling voices of two of the spouses of victims who lived just a few houses away from where I lived with my family. As they told friends and neighbors soon after the calm, their spouses were killed because they weren't in a place of safety. Still, the stories have become embellished or fabricated by those not on the scene.

Exhaustive research was done to ascertain the facts about how each of these nine citizens of Tracy died utilizing newspaper accounts, eyewitnesses, hospital workers, or family members.

Besides Nancy Vlahos, whose death is detailed in the book, the following other eight citizens of Tracy were also killed:

Fred Pilatus, seventy-one, was born in Colorado Springs, Colorado. He was a farmhand and was partially paralyzed in a farm accident six years prior to his death. The injury caused him to use a walker in getting around. When the warning siren was blowing, Albin Holm, a neighbor, along with his grandson, Bob, and a roomer, Hank Smith, ran over to the Pilatus home and offered to help Fred into the basement. Fred stubbornly refused their help and chose to remain on the main floor. His wife, Minnie, told the three men to go into the basement rather than risking their lives by going back home. The three ducked under a heavy table in the basement. Minnie chose to stay with her husband upstairs. Minnie's life was spared, but she was bleeding profusely as she screamed for someone to help her find Fred. Minnie was rushed to the hospital where she was listed in critical condition. Neighbors found Fred partially wrapped in a drape and covered by rubble. Dolly De-Blieck, a nurse who lived across the street, checked his vital signs and pronounced him dead.

Otelia Werner, seventy-five, was born in Elgin, Minnesota. She and her husband, John, moved to Tracy in 1922 and lived three houses west of the Pilatuses. The Werners were checking the weather outside when they heard the civil defense siren. Moments later, they saw the tornado and headed to the basement. Otelia, figuring she had time, decided to go back upstairs to retrieve her purse despite her husband urging her not to. The tornado hit their home before she made it back downstairs. Their home was completely destroyed and Otelia was found halfway down the basement steps with piles of rubble on top of her. She was bleeding profusely and rescue workers could hear her gasping for air. But it took the workers so long to uncover her that she wasn't breathing by the time they got her into an emergency vehicle. She was pronounced dead at the hospital. John received only minor cuts and scrapes. Accounts of the reason why Otelia went back upstairs have varied over the years. John told neighbors and rescue workers soon after the tornado that she went back to get her purse. Other stories told of her going back upstairs to close a window or to retrieve a valuable painting.

Ellen Morgan, seventy-five, was born in Kewanee, Illinois, and moved to Tracy in 1935. Ellen was a widow and was invited to the home of Mariom Nelson that evening for supper. Miriam's daughter. Gertrude Hammersmark and granddaughter, Michele, were also there visiting from Billings, Montana. While sitting at the table finishing the meal, the women heard the warning siren. Mariam thought there was an accident on the highway. With the siren continuing, Gertrude became scared and argued that a tornado was coming and that they should get into the basement. Mariam and Gertrude continued to disagree about why the siren was sounding. Gertrude then decided to head for the basement. Because she had polio, it took her a while to get down the stairs. By the time she reached the basement, the tornado struck the home. Mariam and Michele were headed for the basement, but didn't make it in time and hovered in front of the stove beside the basement steps. Mariam was hit by the refrigerator and suffered five broken ribs. Michele was knocked out momentarily and had a cut on her forehead and several bruises. Gertrude sustained bruised on her arms where she had covered her head. Ellen, in all likelihood, was standing in the kitchen near the basement steps when the tornado struck. She was later found dead under the debris. With Mariam hospitalized, Gertrude identified Ellen's body after it was brought to the hospital.

Barbara Holbrook, fifty, was born in Tracy and lived there her entire life. Barbara was at home with her children, Robert, Lee, Janet, and Janice and her son-in-law, William Barret, in the Greenwood section. All made it safely into the basement, but Barbara thought the tornado had already passed and went back upstairs. The tornado then struck the house and, after a lengthy search, Barbara was found by rescue workers with flashlights in a field nearly 200 yards from her residence. None of the others in the house at the time were injured.

Walter Swanson, forty-seven, was born in Holly Township near Slayton, Minnesota. A farmhand most of his life, he lived in Greenwood with his brother, Louis. When the tornado was approaching, neighbors encouraged Walter, who was outside in his yard, to come to their home for shelter. He looked up at the funnel, shrugged his shoulders and laughed, as if to say it would break up before it reached Greenwood. His home did not include a basement. Walter soon realized, though, that he was in danger and tried to run into a nearby ditch for safety. The tornado leveled his home. Walter was not found until the following morning by rescue workers in a field over 150 yards away from where his home once stood. Walter was the last of the nine declared dead from the devastation.

Ella Haney, eighty-four, was born in Perham, Minnesota. She was a widow and had been living in the Greenwood section of Tracy since 1962. Haney was hard of hearing and required a hearing aid. But she often took the hearing aid out when she slept. She often took naps after her evening meal on the couch. While the warning siren was blaring, rescue workers assumed Ella didn't hear it because she was found her lying dead next to her couch without her hearing aid in. It is believed she died in her sleep.

Mildred Harnden, seventy-five, was born in Canby and had been living in Tracy since 1908. She and her husband, Charles, were at their home in Greenwood when the tornado struck. The Harndens were sitting on their screened-in back porch and were unaware the tornado was rapidly approaching because their house was surrounded by trees. When they finally saw the tornado, the elderly couple, who did not have a basement in their home, realized it was too late to attempt to seek safety at another residence. Charles put his arms around his wife in an attempt to shield her, but the force of the winds blew them both out the back door. Millie was found bleeding heavily with the screen door wrapped around her. She was pronounced dead at the hospital. Charles was treated for numerous injuries, including two broken ribs, a broken leg, and a punctured lung.

Paul Swanson, sixty, was born in Pierre, South Dakota. He moved to Tracy in 1947 and was living in a cabin owned by Sadie Van Dusen north of Tracy. Because there was no storm shelter in the vicinity of the cabin, Swanson got in is car and tried to outrun the tornado. Witnesses say he was heading away from the tornado and it appeared as though he would be safe. But the tornado was seconds from dissipating and began to stagger in all directions like a child's toy top does when it starts to slow up. The tornado switched directions more than once during its final act and struck Swanson's car, rolling it over several times. He was found dead several yards from the car in a rock pile.

While some of the stories about the tornado have been embellished over the years, there is no exaggerating death.

Chapter 13
A TIME TO REFLECT
Winter 2011

A S HARD AS IT WAS TO ADMIT, there were questions I was unable to answer regarding the night of June 13, 1968. The majority of the of the undiscovered lore is entombed for eternity. After numerous trips to Tracy for research, the information I accrued was time consuming, yet rewarding. Now, though, my educational quest was complete.

I felt a little like a parent when a child grows up and moves away from home. I was going to miss talking to old friends and new acquaintances about this particular project. I would miss learning something new every time I contacted someone or researched a certain aspect of the tornado. Nearly everyone was more cooperative than I expected. One or two denied my request to talk about yesteryear for one reason or another, but the overall experience was comforting.

While previously shying away from returning to Tracy since the passing of my parents, I was now certain there would be more return trips. Only now, they would be for personal reasons and not to gather data.

After filling the Blazer with gas for the drive back to Willmar, I turned north off Highway 14 and was now on the familiar Airport Road. It was the same route I had taken for the countless other trips to and from Tracy to converse about the tornado. But this time felt different. I gazed in the rear-view mirror and saw the town gradually disappear as I drove away.

Six miles out of town, I saw the back of the sign on the opposite side of the road. It was the mileage sign that I had stopped at due to a flat tire seven months earlier. This was the spot where I received the tap on my shoulder, much like a light bulb going off in someone's mind when a good idea comes to the forefront, as I changed the tire in light rain. It was here that I thought about the sisters and what they were doing forty-three years after being blown out of their house by the tornado. It was in this exact location where the idea to write the book came to me.

I pulled my vehicle onto to the shoulder, then stopped and looked across the road at the back of the sign for a moment. It stood lonely and swayed gently in the winter breeze. I got out and stood beside the vehicle. This time, I could envision what the baseball players and coach were looking at through the bus windows and how each one felt as the bus motored closer to town.

I could also imagine how Walnut Grove teenager Eric Lantz must have felt when he looked at this horrific twirling monster through his camera outside of town after he and his father arrived on the scene. The young man's pictures were so captivating that he was awarded third place in the 1968 National Newspaper Association contest for best news photo.

As I looked back toward Tracy once more, I felt a sense of pride at how the townspeople helped each other following the catastrophe. It didn't matter what nationality they were. It didn't matter which side of the tracks they lived on. And it didn't matter if they were young or old, wealthy or poor, male or female, or healthy or ill. They helped one another as if they were a family. And because of the close bond the people in this small town formed during this tragic time, they became one big family.

While nearly everyone interviewed had a tornado yarn or two or ten to tell, it was strange that Linda was initially unsure about disclosing the details of her story. She wasn't being uncooperative, but it was mysterious to me how her recollection of that night was dim at first.

Linda's siblings, parents and friends never heard her speak much about the tornado over the years. Even her second husband and their children knew little of the details of that night except what they read. But eventually Linda allowed her suppressed memory to be unharnessed.

Two days after the tornado and one day before she would bury her daughter, Susan Vlahos drove to Tracy to visit Linda in the hospital. Unlike the first time when Susan was denied visiting rights because Linda was in intensive care, she was allowed to meet with her friend.

Because she was heavily sedated at the time, Linda has no memory of Susan coming into her room that day. But almost immediately after entering the room, Susan was deluged with apologies from Linda, who blamed herself for Nancy's death. Susan understood from the stories she heard that there was little Linda could have done to save the little girl's life. Susan repeatedly attempted to convey to Linda that no one was to blame.

But Linda continued to carry the guilt with her for over forty years. She granted an occasional interview to a newspaper writer on the anniversary of the tornado, but not unless she was urged to do so. Even then, she shed little information about that night.

When Linda was approached about having her story documented in *Out of the Blue*, she politely attempted to talk me out of it. My persistence finally persuaded her to relent, although she offered only small dabs of information following a question. When asked to elaborate, she became uncomfortable and fidgeted like a boy in a barber chair.

Pam admitted that her life was an open book, but because of her young age, the details of the storm were not always vivid. She also admitted that she and Linda had never sat down together and talked about the tornado until they were interviewed for *Out of the Blue* at their mother's home in Tracy on November 5.

Linda's sister, Kathy, also mentioned that her older sister rarely spoke to her about that night either. Some of the details revealed during the research for the book were new to the family, even though Linda knew about some of them, she had not offered the information.

It was as though Linda had certain events of that night unconsciously blocked from her memory. Soon, though, the more questions posed to her, the more she remembered and soon became more comfortable talking about them.

The reason for keeping the memories locked up over the years became understandable when she openly admitted still feeling guilty about the little girl's death. She often posed questions to herself such as "What if I hadn't tried to adopt her?" or "What if I had gone to the basement sooner than I did?"

After months of attempting to track down Susan, I finally located her in Hampton, Iowa. After two marriages that ended in divorce, Susan was now retired and living alone in Hampton, Iowa. Just as Linda had answered me when inquired as to why she and Susan had not spoken to one another since the tornado, Susan offered no explanation. There was no bitter fallout between them. It was just one of those things where both parties got wrapped up in other events of their life. Susan, who was engaged at the time of the tornado, got married six months later.

Susan often interrupted my questions to her by asking about Linda's life. I had informed Linda earlier that I had located Susan. And she granted me permission to give out her phone number if Susan requested it.

Two hours after I talked to Susan, my phone rang. It was Linda excitedly informing me that Susan had called and they spoke at length about the friendship they once shared. Linda again told Susan that she felt guilty for Nancy's death. And again Susan made it clear that she held no animosity toward her. Before they discontinued their phone conversation, the women spoke genuinely about staying in touch.

Even though Linda will forever feel somehow responsible for the child's death, she seemed relieved after speaking with Susan. Her voice was more enthusiastic and her demeanor had changed. She had been harboring these dark thoughts for too long and now to hear Susan say she was not to blame was like receiving an antidote.

Linda and Clifford did not have any children before they divorced after four years of marriage. Clifford eventually remarried and currently lives in Nicollet with his wife.

As for the two sisters involved in the tornado, they are now grandmothers. Pam is single and lives and works in Currie, Minnesota. She has five children and three grandchildren.

Linda married Gene Tordsen in 1974. They initially lived in Slayton, Minnesota, where Linda owned and operated a store named Linda's Craftland and Jewelry for seventeen years. They currently live in Sauk Centre where Linda owned the Gold 'n More store for many years before selling her business and retiring last August. She and Gene have two grown children, two grandchildren, and one step-grand-child.

It was evident that Linda never stopped think-ing about Nancy throughout all these years. When she and Gene had their daughter, Jenny, Linda chose Ann for her middle name. And it wasn't until the book was being written that Jenny was told her mid-dle name was selected because it was the same as Nancy's.

Linda never knew the names of the two men who saved her life until she was told during the re-search for the book. When told that they had both passed away, Linda felt sorrow that she would never get a chance to thank them.

Another thing she never knew until it was dis-closed during research for the book was another item of hers that was discovered three days after the tor-nado in Redwood Falls, a city forty-five miles north-east of Tracy.

Ken Hyrunga noticed a torn piece of paper in his farmyard that looked like a child's school tablet with the wide blue-dashed lines. The yellowish-colored paper had been torn apart, with Ken discovering the top third of the page. The edges were frayed, the paper was stained and the ink was smudged from being wet. Ken had heard about a few Redwood Falls residents finding canceled checks from Tracy following the tornado and he wondered if this paper also came from there.

So Ken decided to make a call to Leo Jette, an acquaintance of his in Tracy. He asked Leo to see if he knew anyone with the name written at the top of the letter. Leo said he didn't know but would ask around. Two days later, Leo called Ken back and said his wife, Florence, knew of a hospitalized woman injured in the tornado that could be linked to the letter.

Ken decided it wasn't worth bothering someone in the hospital over a scrap of paper and halted his investigation, tossing the paper away. Now passed away, Ken never knew that the letter was indeed the one Linda was writing to Clifford when the tornado struck.

The portion of the smudged letter he found simply read:

Cliffy,
It's raining and hailing here tonight and the wind is blowing hard . . .

TORNADO MYTHS AND FACTS

According to the Tornado Project based in St. Johnsbury, Vermont, there are several misunderstandings pertaining to tornadoes. With their permission, they allowed *Out of the Blue* to list these five major myths or misconceptions found on their website.

(1) The southwest corner of a basement is the safest location during passage of a tornado.

The truth is that the part of the home towards the approaching tornado (often, but not always, the southwest) is the least safe part of the basement, not the safest. This is also true of the above-ground portion of the house. In tornadoes, many more homes will be shifted than will be blown completely free of a foundation. Homes that are attacked from the southwest tend to shift to the northeast. The unsupported part of the house may then collapse into the basement or pull over part of the foundation, or both. Historically, the few deaths in basements have been caused by collapsed basement walls, houses and chimneys, rather than by debris thrown into the basement from the outside.

For nearly a century, the published conventional wisdom was that the southwest corner of a building, both above and below ground, afforded the best protection. This misconception probably originated from someone's reasoning, rather than from actual observations. They probably assumed that deadly debris would be propelled over the southwest corner and land in the northeast corner.

The idea that it was safe to seek shelter on the side of the house facing the oncoming tornado dates back to at least the first book on tornadoes, the 1887 comprehensive text *Tornadoes*, by John Park Finley. He placed in italic for emphasis the following remark: 'Under no circumstances, whether in a building or in a cellar, ever take a position in a northeast room, in a northeast corner, or an east room, or against an east wall." He also recommended removing the furniture from the west-facing room and closing all windows in the house. This is all incorrect, deadly, and time-wasting advice. It is quite possible that someone has died following it. While relatively few people probably read the book when it was available, the advice was quoted in many newspapers. It is possible that in the limited number of damage surveys Finley conducted personally, he came upon a grisly scene involving the northeast portion of a poorly constructed house that had fallen over, and it strongly influenced his thinking.

These assumption went essentially unchallenged until 1966, when Professor Joseph Eagleman of the University of Kansas undertook a survey of destroyed homes produced by the Topeka tornado of June 8th. Professor Eagleman's objective study showed that the south side and southwest corners, the direction of approach of the Topeka tornado, were the least safe areas, and the north side of homes were the safest — both on the first floor and in the basement. He repeated the study after the Lubbock, Texas, tornado of May 11, 1970, and the results were even more striking. The southwest portion of the houses were unsafe in seventy-five percent of the damaged homes. That was double the percentage of unsafe areas in the northeast part of homes. As a general rule, people in basements will escape injury despite extreme devastation above them. Being under a stairwell, heavy table, or workbench will afford even more protection.

(2) Some towns are "protected."

Many years ago, various Native American tribes perceived tornadoes in different ways. Some saw them as a cleansing agent, sweeping away the ragged and negative things of life. Others saw them as a form of revenge for dishonoring the Great Spirit. Today, only the myths about the protection of towns by rivers and hills linger in modern American culture.

The Osage Indians, native to Kansas, Oklahoma, and Missouri passed on tornado legends to the early settlers. One such legend has it that tornadoes will not strike between two rivers, near the point where rivers join. In the past 150 years, this idea may have given a false sense of security to some people who thereby failed to take shelter. They may not have lived to help debunk the myth. One by one, the myths that particular towns are protected have fallen by the wayside.

Emporia, Kansas, for instance, had sat "protected' between the Cottonwood and Neosho rivers, in native Osage territory, for over a century. Emporia was free of damaging tornadoes until June 8, 1974 when a tornado killed six people and destroyed twenty million dollars worth of property on the northwest side of town. Another tornado caused six million dollars in damage along the west side of Emporia on June 7, 1990. Part of the path of the 1974 tornado was also the site of a deadly twister on September 29, 1881, but the area was farmland at that time.

The idea that one's town in "protected" is a combination of wishful thinking, short memory, the rarity of tornadoes, and distorted sense of "here" and "there." Proof of protection has been offered by a very simple statement of fact. The town has never been hit by a tornado, but ten tornadoes have touched own outside of town in the past thirty years. The occurrence information may be fact, but the conclusion that the town must be "protected" does not logically follow.

That logic disregards some very basic ideas. It ignores the likely possibility that rivers, ridges, and valleys have little or no effect on mature tornadoes. Tornadoes have passed seemingly unaffected over mountain ridges three thousand feet high. Dozens have crossed the Mississippi River, from Minnesota to Louisiana. Both sides of the river, at the confluence of the Mississippi and Missouri Rivers, near St. Louis, have seen devastating tornadoes.

Topography may have some influence, but protection is not one of them. Weak tornadoes may damage hilltops. But well-formed, mature tornadoes may actually stretch themselves into valleys and intensify.

During this vortex stretching, the funnel diameter may shrink in diameter and the tornado will spin even more rapidly. This is hardly what one would call protection for buildings in a valley.

The belief that tornadoes don't hit "here," but always seem to hit "north of town" or "south of the river" ignores some very simple mathematics. "Here" may be a small town with an area of one square mile. Just "outside of town" or "to the north" may be anywhere within visual sighting from the water tower, perhaps ten miles in all directions. Therefore, if the town has an area of one square mile, then "outside of town" has an area over 300 square miles. A tornado touchdown is 300 times more likely "outside" of town than in-town. The "protection" of the town does not come from hills, or a mound, or the joining of two rivers. Tornado protection comes from that same source as our protection from falling comets or heavenly visitors—that afforded by the laws of probability—the very low probability of rare events such as tornadoes.

(3) Tornadoes never strike big cities.

This misconception has a small kernel of possible truth at its heart. Before we get to that possible bit of truth, we first have to make a number of things clear. When one thinks of a big city, the image of skyscrapers and large office or apartment buildings comes to mind. In actuality, if you were to compare the downtown where these buildings occur with the rest of the city, it would comprise a rather small percentage of the city's area. That more cities aren't struck by tornadoes is probably more coincidence than anything else. There are very few big cities with skyscrapers in Tornado Alley. In fact, there are only a dozen, and one of them, St. Louis, Missouri, has a history of tornadoes in its central area. A tornado passed through Miami, Florida, in 1997 before it moved out to sea, disproving the idea that tornadoes can't form in cities. In the past forty years, the city of St. Louis and the surrounding suburbs of St. Louis County have been hit twenty-two times, although none of them were in the tiny skyscraper heart of the city. There are three possible reasons for that. First, the central city may produce a "heat island" in which turbulent rising air disrupts the formation of small tornadoes (keep in mind that the majority of tornadoes are small). The second possibility is that the roughness created by the skyscrapers causes turbulence that disrupts the formation of small tornadoes. The third is that tornadoes are rare and the central city is very small. So it is a matter of coincidence.

Professor Tetsuya Fujita of the University of Chicago suggested that the "heat island" effect takes hold for small tornadoes when a city reaches a population of about one million. There seems to be a lack of small tornadoes in the central cities of Chicago, Tokyo, and London. These are the only three cities that have been carefully studied over a long time.

None of this applies to intense tornadoes. They are just too rare to assume that they avoid central cities. There are thousands of small towns across Tornado Alley that have never been hit by an intense tornado. Perhaps some time in the next century, a central city will be in the path of a violent tornado, and we will learn what will happen. The probability of a violent tornado in the downtown area of any large city is about one in a thousand years.

It is possible that a tornado could actually intensify even more after it forms outside of town and moves into the central city. One speculation is that the friction of the buildings will slow down the inflow of air into the funnel. This would deprive the funnel of air. The pressure would drop, causing the funnel to shrink in diameter, and spin even faster. So central-city tornadoes that begin outside the city could be more damaging than average.

(4) Opening windows to equalize air pressure will save a roof, or even a home, from destruction from a tornado.

The idea that by moving one thin pane of glass is going to protect a roof or home from one of the most violent forces of nature on the planet has a certain amount of absurdity about it. In reality, opening windows is a dangerous and useless waste of time, and could actually be harmful to the house.

To get to the very center of a mature tornado — where the pressure may be low enough to cause some explosive effects — the windows would have to endure 100- to 200-mile-per-hour winds in the wall of the vortex.

Those winds would be laden with boards, stones, cars, trees, telephone poles, and the neighbor's roof shingles, as well as wind pressure of more than 100 pounds per square foot. This barrage would blow more than enough ventilation holes in the building to allow any pressure difference to be equalized.

Even with the windows closed, most houses and commercial buildings have enough openings to vent the pressure in the time that it takes for a tornado to pass. The engineering team at Texas Tech's Institute of Disaster Research pointed out that the pressure drop inside a tornado with 260-mile-per-hour winds is only about ten percent, or just 1.4 pounds per square inch. Most buildings can vent this difference through its normal openings in about three seconds. That is sufficient time even if the tornado is moving forward at a very rapid sixty miles per hour.

If the homeowner opens the wrong window, air can rush in and exert pressure on the structure from the inside, similar to blowing air into a balloon. It is unlikely that the resident knows where the weak points of construction are in a house. In addition, the wind fields in a passing tornado are very complex and constantly changing. It is not possible to predict the strongest direction of attack. The best advice is to leave the windows alone and get into the basement or other shelter as quickly as possible.

(5) Highway overpasses are a safe place to shelter if you are on the road when you see a tornado coming.
In a film entitled *Terrible Tuesday*, about the Wichita Falls, Texas, tornado of 1979, a man was interviewed by a reporter about his close brush with death. He had been on the highway when he realized a tornado was coming. He parked his car and ran up underneath the overpass crossing the highway. In the early 1990s, the television crew covering a story was on the way back from the shoot. They saw a tornado, and when they realized it was gaining on them, they parked the car and ran up under the overpass, where several other people had tried to take shelter. A small tornado was headed straight for them, but tossed around a van before it reached them. The weak tornado then passed south of them, but both the experience and the video they shot were intense. The video was shown on television programs and newscasts across the nation.

Since the video clip aired, many people have come to assume that this is a safe shelter. But this is a modern-day myth. Scientists, meteorologists and the emergency management people have become very frustrated with the increasing number of motorists taking shelter in an overpass. The fact is that any time you deliberately put yourself above ground level during a tornado, you are putting yourself in harm's way.

During the May 3, 1999, Oklahoma tornadoes, dozens of motorists pulled over on the highway and ran up under highway overpasses. Not only did they put themselves at risk, but they put many other motorists at risk by blocking the roads in the area of the overpass.

Tornado Facts

The most powerful tornadoes occur in the United States. Tornado winds are the most powerful winds on Earth.

A tornado has been reported in all fifty states.

Every tornado has its own color, shape, and sound.

Although a tornado can strike at any time, most occur between 3:00 p.m. And 9:00 p.m.

The chances that a tornado is an EF5, the highest classification on the scale, is less than 0.1 percent.

Some tornadoes make a considerable amount of noise, while other make very little noise. It all depends on the objects a tornado might come in contact with or carry. A tornado moving along an open plain, for example, will make very little noise.

The deadliest tornado happened in 1925. It swept through three states, killing 695 people and injuring over 2,000. The Tri-State tornado traveled 219 miles through parts of Illinois, Indiana, and Missouri.

Minnesota Tornado Facts

Many other historic weather conditions occurred in Minnesota in 1968 besides the first F5 tornado in state history that pummeled Tracy.

Just north of Truman, in the south central part of the state, the earliest recorded tornado in Minnesota state history occurred on March 18, 1968. The latest tornado was November 16, 1931, near Maple Plain in east central Minnesota.

The state's largest hail stone, six inches in circumference, was recorded in Edgerton in the southwest portion of the state on July 4, 1968.

The deadliest tornado in Minnesota history occurred on April 14, 1886. The tornado struck at 4:00 p.m. It razed parts of St. Cloud and Sauk Rapids. Seventy-two people were killed and 213 injured. Among those killed were eleven members of a wedding party, including the groom.

Besides the tornado that struck Tracy, there has been only one other F5 or EF5 tornado recorded in Minnesota. Chandler was hit at 4:00 p.m. on June 16, 1992. There was one death and thirty-five injured in that tornado.

ACKNOWLEDGEMENTS

T HE INFORMATION GATHERED FOR THIS BOOK could not have been made possible without the assistance of many caring individuals and businesses.

First, Linda Tordsen and Pam Haugen had their memories pushed to the brink continually, even when it came to minor details such as what they ate, what they saw and what they said at certain times forty-three years ago. I have trouble remembering those things an hour later. Both of these two wonderful women cooperated fully and I am thankful it was not their time to go in 1968.

Numerous others assisted me with locating people involved with the tornado, answering questions, donating photos, etc.

A former high school classmate of mine, Steve Almlie, was especially gracious in helping with the completion of this book. Even during his busy times, he did whatever he could to assist me.

Karen Peterson of the Wheels Across the Prairie Museum in Tracy always seemed to go above and beyond the call of duty for me. If I asked for one name or one photo, she gave me three.

Eric Lantz, whose help with the book was twofold, took several outstanding pictures of the tornado. He graciously allowed me to use his award-winning photo for the cover of my book. Lantz is now a staff radiologist, Diagnostic Radiology at the Mayo Clinic in Rochester, Minnesota. He also assisted in explaining some of the medical terminology for the book.

Bernie Holm, the former fire chief and civil defense director in Tracy, gave me a minute-by-minute description of how he and his crew on the fire department dealt with the tragedy.

Seth Schmidt, the publisher of the *Tracy Headlight Herald*, and his staff were also extremely helpful with information and pictures. They never balked at any of my numerous requests and ended each response with, "Let me know if there is anything else I can help you with." Seth also took time out of his busy schedule to write one of the forewords for my book.

Jerrid Sebesta, whom I covered as a high school and college standout basketball as a daily newspaper sports editor, also was kind enough to accept my offer and write a foreword. It's no surprise that Jerrid is an excellent meteorologist at KARE-11 TV. At six-foot-six, the Montevideo, Minnesota, native has a better view of the weather than most of his colleagues.

Laurie Ebbers and others at the Nobles County Library in Worthington dug deep into the historical archives time and time again to come up with as much information as she could. She provided me with addresses, records, obituaries, and photos from people and places in Worthington.

Jenni Broyles, an Extreme Stormchaser from Alabama whom I met during work on the book, provided me with valuable information about tornadoes.

The following are the many other individuals and groups that, without their help, I would be still be laboring to find the light at the end of the tunnel.

Robert Aguilera
John Almlie
Vera Anderson
Pam Baumann
Bill Bolin
Jenna Blum
Rhonda Christoffers
Jeremy Den Hartog
Jenny Dreger
Missie Erbes
Vernon Grinde
Michele Hammersmark
Betty Haugen
Chuck Haugen
Clarence Haugen
Kathy Haugen Peterson
Lois Johnson
Maggie Kamholz
Allan Koch
Bruce Koch
Janette Koch
Curt Jette
Susan (Vlahos) Madera
Art Peterson

Marie Sanow
Hillary Sass
Joseph Sass
Jerrid Sebesta
Meribel Steiner
Harriet Timmerman
Rodney Timmerman
Heather Thoma
Clifford Vaske
Dolores Vaske
Kelli Vogel
Katherine Ziemke
City of Tracy
Lyon County Historical Society
Marshall Independent
Minneapolis Tribune (now *Minneapolis StarTribune*)
Minnesota State Climatology Office
Minnesota State Historical Society
National Weather Service - Chanhassen, Minnesota Bureau
Nobles County Historical Society
Nobles County Library
Redwood Falls Gazette
Sanford Tracy Hospital
St. Paul Pioneer Press
The Tornado Project
Tracy Chamber of Commerce
United State Census Bureau
Walnut Grove Tribune (now *Westbrook Sentinel-Tribune*)
Worthington Daily Globe